18 MAR 1997

£14-99

HM 20 CRY

KT-148-510

# THE RESEARCH STUDENT'S GUIDE TO SUCCESS

WITHDRAWN

LIBRARY
EDUCATION CENTRE
PRINCESS ROYAL HOSPITAL

TELFORD

CB008659

# THE RESEARCH STUDENT'S GUIDE TO SUCCESS

## PAT CRYER

LIBRARY
EDUCATION CENTRE
PRINCESS ROYAL HOSPITAL

**Open University Press**
Buckingham · Philadelphia

Open University Press
Celtic Court
22 Ballmoor
Buckingham
MK18 1XW

and
1900 Frost Road, Suite 101
Bristol, PA 19007, USA

First Published 1996
Reprinted 1996

Copyright © Pat Cryer 1996

All rights reserved. Except for the quotation of short passages for the
purpose of criticism and review, no part of this publication may be
reproduced, stored in a retrieval system, or transmitted, in any form or
by any means, electronic, mechanical, photocopying, recording or
otherwise, without the prior written permission of the publisher or a
licence from the Copyright Licensing Agency Limited. Details of such
licences (for reprographic reproduction) may be obtained from the
Copyright Licensing Agency Ltd of 90 Tottenham Court Road, London,
W1P 9HE.

A catalogue record of this book is available from the British Library

ISBN 0 335 19611 X (pb)  0 335 19612 8 (hb)

**Library of Congress Cataloging-in-Publication Data**
Cryer, Pat.
    The research student's guide to success / Pat Cryer.
        p.   cm.
    Includes bibliographical references and index.
    ISBN 0–335–19612–8.    ISBN 0–335–19611–X (pbk.)
    1. Study skills—Great Britain.   2. Doctor of philosophy degree—
Great Britain.   3. Report writing—Great Britain.
    4. Dissertations, Academic—Great Britain.   5. Graduate students—
Great Britain.   6. Research—Great Britain.   I. Title.
LB2395.C787   1996
378.1'702812—dc20                                        95–25351
                                                              CIP

Typeset by Graphicraft Typesetters Limited, Hong Kong
Printed in Great Britain by St Edmundsbury Press,
Bury St Edmunds, Suffolk

LIBRARY
EDUCATION CENTRE
PRINCESS ROYAL HOSPITAL

# CONTENTS

# FOREWORD

So you want to do a research degree? This is a hard question and without knowing more about what it entails, most students have only a very hazy idea about exactly what is involved in doing a research degree. This is hardly surprising; compare the volume of information available in university prospectuses on the content and teaching of taught courses with that on research degrees. But students are not the only ones in the dark. The government itself recently undertook a consultation inviting views on 'the nature of the PhD', and I have taught on a number of courses for research student supervisors where this question was asked, leading to animated discussions with as many different views as there were people in the room.

You might expect that supervisors would provide all the necessary advice on the nature of research work, but, according to research by Susan Hetrick and Vernon Trafford of Anglia Business School, many supervisors expect students to start with a clear idea of the problem at hand and of what they want to do. This may be unrealistic, because the skills required for research are very different from those needed for undergraduate work. Undergraduates tend to work on problems for which a correct answer exists or has at least been defined, but in research work the problem may not in fact have an answer, and there may be few if any academic sources of help. You are moving from a degree where many students are taught by a number of different academics to a personal course which is guided, rather than taught, by one or two supervisors. On an undergraduate course, work is divided into manageable chunks with set targets and deadlines, whereas on a research degree there is only one examination several years down the line with only a few formal progress reports in between. There is a shift in responsibility for progress from tutor to student; you must learn to manage your work effectively and to set your own goals. Many supervisors will set goals for you in the early stages, but it is a sign of maturity in the research process when you can start to do it for yourself.

Research by its very nature breaks new ground, so that as your course progresses you will become the expert in your area of work, and will come to know more about it than your supervisor. This means that you will have to take your own initiatives – you will have to decide the best course of action, while your supervisor gradually assumes less of a guiding role. As the former Science and Engineering Research Council guide put it, you will start as master and pupil and end as almost equal colleagues.

As well as taking more responsibility for the course of the work, you will also have to make the running on issues such as research training. For many years it was assumed that research students would pick up their research skills from their supervisors with little or no formal training. More recently, many institutions have been introducing some training courses in research skills, but the individual nature of research work still means that individual students have to take a role in defining the skills they need. Being forewarned about what skills will be needed later in the research programme will help you to ensure that you are able to receive suitable training when the time comes.

It is these sorts of issue that this book addresses. It provides an invaluable guide not only to the research degree itself, but more importantly to the range of skills required to progress through it successfully. It examines the whole process from the reasons for undertaking a research degree to the final examination and after, including along the way advice on such things as how to make presentations and how to ensure an audience for them! Many people claim that innovation cannot be taught – it must be picked up from the supervisor by some form of osmosis – but the author makes good use of her background both in science and mathematics and in educational research to dispel such myths with a useful chapter on creative thinking. The book also includes advice on the more personal areas of research work such as dealing with the block of depression which seems to hit most research students with about a year to go, when it seems as if the work done to date will never produce a valid thesis. Rest assured, it almost always does!

One of the most pleasing aspects of this book is that it attempts to inform the reader about the processes involved in research degrees while recognizing the vital fact that, given the diversity of students and supervisors, there is no single valid method or 'right' way.

A research degree is the academic equivalent of scaling an unclimbed peak. It requires skill, determination and lots of hard work, but when you do get to the top you have the knowledge that you have done something no one else has done before. Very few people who have completed a research degree ever regret having done so. I hope that you, too, will have a rewarding experience.

*James Irvine*
*Chair, National Postgraduate Committee, 1993–95*

# PREFACE

This book has grown out of numerous enjoyable and stimulating encounters with research students and their supervisors. It started with my being invited into Birkbeck College, University of London, to research and develop a self-study booklet customized for its own postgraduate research students. The topic was to be ways in which the postgraduate research students could facilitate their own progress, irrespective of the discipline area.

I liked the idea of the work at Birkbeck. I had experience of gathering and processing information from interviews; I had supervised research students and contributed to research student training while at the University of Surrey; I had considerable experience in developing self-study materials; and I had the advantage of an academic background in both the natural and the social sciences. Furthermore, I had for years been convinced that research students needed something akin to, but additional to, the study skills that had proved effective at undergraduate and taught masters levels. Although these additional skills often did develop naturally and 'rub off' by the end of a research programme, I felt intuitively that the whole process of being a research student could be made more effective and enjoyable if they could be systematically identified and then formally presented to research students for them to internalize and develop at an early stage. An added benefit ought to be a bringing down of completion times to within the three to four years normally aimed at for doctoral research.

I also suspected that there might be a hitherto unrecognized scope and richness to what I saw as this body of 'something' akin to study skills for research students. I saw it as just waiting to be teased out from existing but as yet disconnected research studies and from the experience and knowledge of the countless individuals who had been research students or supervisors. I felt privileged and stimulated at being in the position of seeing if it could be done, and, if so, of processing the results into a meaningful whole that would be practically useful. An umbrella term needed to be coined for this 'something' that I was envisaging. 'Work strategies' alone would have encapsulated the idea, but it did not carry a unique meaning that is generally and immediately recognized. 'Study skills' does carry such a meaning. So I coined the term 'work strategies and study skills'.

This book on work strategies and study skills for postgraduate research students is based on the Birkbeck studies and on additional ones at the Bartlett School of the Built Environment at University College London, and at Roehampton Institute London. It has also benefited from my involvement at various levels of formality with staff and students in higher education institutions in three continents; from my membership of an advisory panel on good supervisory practice of the Engineering and Physical Sciences Research Council; and from the Postgraduate Network of the Society for Research into Higher Education which I convene. I have learnt a great deal from the work of the National Postgraduate Committee of which I am a fervent admirer. I am thus particularly pleased that James Irvine, its Chair (1993–95), has written the Foreword for the book.

A widely held criticism of study skills books is that they give advice on what to do but do not help readers to consider the advice thoughtfully, adapt it for their own needs and then internalize it so that it becomes second nature. It is to meet such criticisms that this book is in self-study format, with activities to help readers to customize the material for their own use. A feature of the self-study format is its conversational style, and I have quite intentionally preserved this. I wanted to do everything possible to make the book easy to interact with and to pick up and put down in odd moments. This may give the superficial appearance of over-simplifying issues which are complex, and of patronizing the reader. I can only say that the majority of research students with whom I have worked have preferred it this way. In particular, they accept that as they travel along paths suggested in the book, they will inevitably find obstacles and challenges for which the book has not prepared them, and that they need to deal with these themselves with the help and support of their supervisors, the resources of their departments and other people in their lives. So this book is essentially practical; although it does represent the results of research, the place for presenting that research is elsewhere (Cryer, 1996).

To add interest to the self-study format, there are boxes throughout, which contain illustrative anecdotes, extracts and quotations. These are either fully referenced in the References section or are so widely known for their sources to be lost or to need no reference.

Although this book is primarily for research students, it should also be of value indirectly to supervisors, in that it should free up supervisor–student contact time from peripheral matters to those relating more directly to research and scholarship in the field of study concerned. The book should also be of value to undergraduate, diploma and taught masters students doing projects and dissertations.

My work with work strategies and study skills for research students has never yet palled. There is always more to learn, which in some ways makes this book published before it is ready, irrespective of its actual publication date. Nevertheless, it represents my answer to regular and earnest requests from research students that I should give them something in writing, urgently, to keep beside them as a ready reference. There are still many opportunities for improvement through practical use; so I would very much appreciate suggestions for the next edition.

*Pat Cryer*
*Higher Education Research and Development Unit,*
*University College London*
January 1996

# ACKNOWLEDGEMENTS

A great many people have contributed to this book – far too many to mention by name. I am grateful to them all and thank them sincerely.

# 1 INTRODUCTION

*Fortune favours the prepared mind.*
(Louis Pasteur, address given on the inauguration of the
Faculty of Science, University of Lille, 7 December 1854)

## The rationale for this book

A research degree should be fascinating and fulfilling, packed with intellectual excitement. If this is to be your experience as a research student, you need to appreciate that ways of working that proved effective at undergraduate and taught masters degree level, important as they still are, are no longer enough. Additional ways need to be developed. This book introduces them, as collected from research students and supervisors in a number of departments and institutions of higher education, and it refers to them under the umbrella term 'work strategies and study skills'.

## The intended reader

As a postgraduate research student or a prospective one, you should find this book useful, irrespective of your research topic, field of study, stage of work or institutional attachment, be it in the United Kingdom or anywhere where English is the language of instruction. The book will also be useful to a more limited extent if you are an undergraduate, taught masters or diploma student doing a research or a research and development project requiring a dissertation.

Some parts of the book will be more relevant for you than others. One reason is that to do its job properly, the book has to be designed for the hypothetical research student who needs a great deal of guidance, help and support throughout the entire research programme and who has a very wide range of uncertainties. You are not such a person. You bring to your work your own individual background, experience and needs. Also, although the advice in the book does have a wide applicability, it is not made up of absolute rights and wrongs, and there is no reason why you should not reject what does not seem likely to be helpful and use or adapt what does.

You may possibly assume or be persuaded that the book must be of limited use to you or any other research student because it is interdisciplinary, and the needs and requirements of each discipline are different from those of any other. To dismiss the book on this basis would be a mistake. Although it is unquestionably true that the requirements and needs of the various disciplines are different, this is largely a matter of terminology and emphasis. Where fundamental differences do exist, the book points them out. So, irrespective of the interdisciplinary basis, provided that you continually bear in mind that your task is to interpret the advice for your own needs, you should find it very useful. Certainly this was the case for the research students from a range of disciplines who worked with pre-published versions.

The book is written primarily from the perspective of the United Kingdom because that is where the main contributing studies were conducted. However, this does not necessarily severely limit its usefulness if you are at an institution outside the United Kingdom. Differences do exist for research students in different countries and cultures, but they too are largely a matter of terminology and emphasis. An example of different terminology could be the terms 'postgraduate student' and 'supervisor' as used in the United Kingdom, which are equivalent to the terms 'graduate student' and 'adviser' as used in certain other English-speaking countries. Some examples of different emphases might be: the component of assessed taught coursework in the otherwise research degree; the administrative structure of the supervision; and the form or even existence of the oral/viva examination. Yet the process of research is essentially the same world-wide; so is interacting effectively with people whom researchers have to work with. So, provided that you accept the task of interpreting the terminology and modifying the emphases, you should find the book useful irrespective of the country in which you are studying.

## How the book is designed

A criticism of many study skills books is that they merely give advice; they do not help readers to adapt the advice for their own personal requirements or to internalize it so that its use becomes second nature. To overcome this criticism, this book provides frequent activities with spaces to indicate that some form of response is required. The purpose of the activities is to help readers to apply the suggested skills and strategies to their own personal circumstances. You may prefer to do the activities in your head, or simply read through them, or even omit them altogether – each of these options is entirely acceptable. If you would find it helpful to respond in writing, make notes in the spaces provided. For lengthier written responses, use separate sheets of paper, which could usefully be kept together in a dedicated file.

You will be able to do many of the activities as you come to them, but some require talking to someone who may not be there, or referring to something which may not be to hand. In these situations, think about what the responses might be, mark the pages for returning to later and continue reading.

You may find it helpful to work through the book with other research students. They need not be working in the same field because the study skills and work strategies are independent of discipline or field of study. In fact, as later chapters will consider more fully, there are many good reasons for developing the habit of working in groups and forging links with researchers in other disciplines.

## How the book is sequenced

The order of early chapters is roughly that in which research students or prospective research students are likely to need them. So, whereabouts in the book you will want to start will depend on how far you are into your research programme. For example, prospective research students who have not yet registered will want to start at Chapter 2; research students who have registered but not yet started will want to start with Chapters 3 and 4; and research students who are close to completion may merely want to read the final chapters.

If you are a fairly new research student, a good way to get the best from the book could be to study the early chapters in detail and just scan the later ones, to get a feel for the type of advice that is in them. As your research programme progresses, your detailed requirements for later chapters will develop somewhat in parallel. Nevertheless, some later chapters will repay early study. For example, Chapters 15 and 16 on originality and creativity come fairly late because they relate particularly to passing through probationary barriers – in the United Kingdom upgrading registration to a doctorate from a research masters. Although probationary barriers normally occur some way into a research programme, it is never too

4 The research student's guide to success

early to start thinking about them, firstly because originality and creativity invariably require lengthy incubation time, and secondly because once you are used to using creative thinking techniques, you will find all sorts of situations where they are helpful. Similarly, it is never too early to start thinking about writing the thesis, which is the subject of Chapter 18.

As you study later chapters, it will probably also be useful to return to earlier ones, because your developing experience will enable you to recognize and appreciate insights which were overlooked on first reading.

## What the book does not do

It is important at the outset to be clear about what the book does not do:

- The book does not consider work strategies and study skills which should already have been developed during undergraduate or taught masters degree work, especially as research students are necessarily deemed good enough to progress to a research degree. (If you feel that you need a refresher course, there is no shortage of useful books. See, for example, those in the Further Reading section at the end of the book.)
- The book does not consider research design. It goes no further than providing pointers on what could contribute to good research. Much more than this is needed for a research degree. A research design needs to be considered and refined over time, through face-to-face discussion with people who know all the aspects and ramifications of the work and who are experienced researchers in the field. These people are first and foremost supervisors and other members of the department, and members of the research group where one exists. These people are close to the work of the research students in their care, and their advice must always take precedence over anything in this book. Some essential, albeit basic, reading on research design for all research students, irrespective of field of study, is suggested in the Further Reading section.
- Where the administrative procedures associated with working for a research degree shape the work strategies and study skills required, this book touches on them. It does no more. Administrative procedures always vary somewhat from department to department, from institution to institution and from country to

country, so do not rely on this book for them. Always check the current position in your own institution.

- Finally, the book does not provide coverage of topics which ought to be on a curriculum for all research students, irrespective of their field of study, such as research ethics, intellectual copyright and, where relevant, health and safety.

In summary, the book is firmly and solely concerned with work strategies and study skills for research students, irrespective of their research topic or field of study.

## Developing and refining your work strategies and study skills

Understanding the need for work strategies and study skills, and knowing what they are, are the two first steps towards developing them, but they are only first steps. You need to practise them continuously, think about how well they are working for you, adapt them to suit you better and then keep on practising them. This cannot be emphasized enough.

# 2 REGISTERING FOR A RESEARCH DEGREE

*Look before you leap.*

(Proverb)

## The importance of starting out right

A research degree is an undertaking of several years. If this time is to be enjoyable as well as profitable, it is essential to start out confident that a research degree is the right course of action for you. Then it is essential to be sure that you will be working on a topic that suits you, with a suitable supervisor and in a department and institution that meets as many as possible of your various needs and expectations. This chapter gives pointers for prospective research students to help them make effective decisions on such matters and take appropriate actions. They are no more than pointers. Departmental and institutional regulations differ widely and no book could possibly give them all. Even those which the book does indicate may no longer be current by the time you read them. So use this chapter to identify issues and as a stimulus for getting up-to-date information from appropriate sources.

## Essential reasons for doing a research degree

Very few people do anything for a single reason, and deciding to do a research degree is no exception. Reasons may be many and varied, but it is useful to think about them in terms of those which are essential for success and those which are merely supporting reasons.

The reasons that are essential for success are those that will sustain during the years ahead. They are almost certainly all intellectual ones: developing a trained mind; satisfying intellectual curiosity;

experiencing an academic community; contributing to knowledge; fulfilling a lifelong ambition; etc. If you do not have reasons such as these for wishing to do a research degree, you should think again about whether it is the right way forward for you. Many research students who register for 'wrong' reasons develop the 'right' ones over time, and become strongly committed to academic values by the time they complete their research programmes. On the other hand, many of them never complete.

## Supporting reasons for doing a research degree

Supporting reasons for wanting to do a research degree in the United Kingdom tend to differ according to whether the individuals concerned are United Kingdom residents or from overseas.

In the United Kingdom unemployment is a major consideration. Jobs are scarce, and individuals newly graduated from first degrees or made redundant from existing jobs can feel that a research degree is a constructive use of time while waiting for the employment situation to improve. This may be so, but counter-arguments ought also to be considered. Even with enhanced earning prospects and grants, bursaries, scholarships or other awards, individuals need luck on their side if they are ever to do more than recoup the expenses of a research degree and the associated loss of earnings. Furthermore, although employers in some areas do like to employ holders of doctorates, perhaps because the work is at the frontiers of knowledge, most, given the option, prefer cheaper first-degree graduates or holders of taught masters degrees. Employers can then afford to provide further training themselves, customized to their own requirements.

Some employers sponsor employees, with no loss of earnings, to do research degrees, usually part-time, in areas that support the work of the employer. Such individuals are fortunate and have a sound supporting reason for doing a research degree.

A common reason for individuals from overseas wanting to do a research degree in the United Kingdom is that they are sponsored by their government or some other agency to help meet the needs of their country. This can be an excellent opportunity to enhance themselves while at the same time having a stimulating cultural experience with all expenses paid. Another reason can be that the home country does not look likely to be a comfortable place for the next few years. Reasons like these are powerful, but counter-considerations should be borne in mind before final decisions are taken. Many people from overseas are used to lifestyles that may not be accessible to them in the United Kingdom. For example, families may find that the accommodation available to them in university towns in the United Kingdom is quite inadequate compared with what they are used to.

(■) **Activity**

What are your own reasons for wanting to do a research degree? Be as specific as possible.

Which of these reasons fit into the category of an 'essential reason' (see above)?

(■) **Discussion of activity**

It cannot be stressed sufficiently that, to be successful, research students need to be motivated by reasons which are, in part at least, intellectual. If you honestly do not have such reasons, or do not think them likely to develop, you would be storing up trouble for yourself by going ahead with a research degree. This should not, however, paint too negative a picture. The lifestyle of (full-time) research students is flexible and individuals are very much their own boss, which most people find fulfilling.

As a prospective research student, you may well be fortunate enough to have had a foretaste of what being a research student is like from the project work that is part of many undergraduate courses. This should help you to decide whether or not being a research student is for you. (■)

## Choosing an institution

A number of factors contribute to decisions about where to register for a research degree, and their relative importance is a matter of individual preference. Factors, in no particular order, include the following:

- Where a bursary, grant, scholarship or other award is offered for research in the field of study of one's choice. (Funding is considered more fully later.)
- Where the structure of the research degree particularly fits in with one's professional experience and/or current employment needs. (Various structures of research degrees are considered later.)
- Where a group of friends or compatriots are registered. This ensures the ongoing support of friends and – particularly for overseas students – social interaction in their own language. (How far this may be beneficial is considered in Chapter 3.)
- Where one did one's first degree. One knows the department, which makes it easy to have informal exploratory discussions with the admissions tutor and prospective supervisors, and one knows the locality and has friends there.
- Where one can live particularly cheaply, either in one's family or with friends.
- Where there are attractive extramural facilities. Theatres, museums and galleries, for example, are most accessible from city institutions; whereas some types of sporting activity may be more accessible from rural and coastal institutions.
- Where the department appears particularly caring towards its research students. (The first obvious sign of this may show up in fast and personalized responses to exploratory letters.)
- Where there is an internationally renowned research group in the proposed field of study. (Such groups are probably already known to prospective research students; if not, they can be identified by recommendation or by checking through relevant research journals. In the United Kingdom these groups tend to exist mainly in what are called 'old' universities. 'New' universities came into existence after the early 1990s, when certain other institutions became universities. Traditionally most research took place in 'old' universities, but many 'new' universities are making impressive headway in terms of overcoming their lack of research tradition by setting up well-considered procedures, seeking additional resources for research, appointing staff from old universities, and setting up various forms of support for their research students and supervisors. Research degrees are also offered by certain institutions

which are not or not yet universities; they are always linked with
a university which oversees their work and gives its name to their
degrees.)
- Where one is already employed, so that one can take advantage
  of reduced fees for employees. (This may involve being supervised
  by a close colleague, which can bring its own problems as well as
  benefits.)
- Where there is a graduate school. (The existence of a graduate
  school does demonstrate that an institution has given thought
  and resources to research degree work, but it demonstrates little
  else. Graduate schools differ markedly in structure and responsibility, and some excellent institutions do not have one.)

The first step in choosing an institution is to think carefully about
relative priorities of these types of consideration. Then write off for
and study the postgraduate prospectus of a number of likely institutions. Contact addresses should be available in public libraries and
libraries of higher and further educational establishments. Overseas
students can use the British Council to find out about institutions
offering research degrees in the United Kingdom.

(■)   **Activity**

---

Using the above considerations to stimulate your thinking, what are
you particularly looking for in your choice of institution for your
research degree?

---

### Choosing the type of research degree

In the United Kingdom there are two common types of research
degree: a doctoral degree and a masters degree. In most institutions
the former is called the Doctor of Philosophy, irrespective of whether
or not the field of study is in fact philosophy, and it is referred to as
the PhD. This is the term used in this book, although some universities do adopt other names for their doctoral degrees (e.g. DPhil).

For administrative purposes, a PhD is assumed to take approximately three years of full-time study, although whether this is in fact the case for any individual research student will depend on a number of factors, which are considered in detail in later chapters. The common masters degree by research is the Master of Philosophy, or MPhil, and in most institutions it is assumed for administrative purposes to take approximately two years of full-time study. Both degrees may be taken on a part-time basis and are then assumed to take correspondingly longer.

Some institutions allow enrolment directly on to a PhD programme. Almost all United Kingdom institutions require their research students to register for an MPhil, even if aiming for a PhD, although applicants who already hold a higher degree from a United Kingdom university in a relevant subject may be permitted to register directly for a PhD. Provided that the quality of a research student's work turns out to be good enough, registration can normally be upgraded and backdated to that for a PhD. Upgrading is not an automatic process. There are various aspects to it, which will be considered in later chapters.

## Choosing the structure of research degree

In the United Kingdom, by far the most common structure or route through an MPhil or PhD is by research, written up as a thesis. Attendance at seminars, taught masters courses, etc. may be a requirement, but is seldom examined and seldom contributes to the final degree.

Other structures are common outside the United Kingdom, and there are now proposals to adopt similar structures within the United Kingdom, to make research degrees more accessible and to address dissatisfaction with completion rates. Some of these structures are already in operation in some institutions. All consist of shortening the content of the thesis and the weight of its contribution to the final degree, and compensating with a mix of other requirements, such as taught modules relating to research; a portfolio of evidence of professional experience and achievement; essays and projects; and peer-reviewed research articles. If you would seriously like such a structure for your research degree, possibly because you have relevant experience to contribute or because taught courses fit better into your lifestyle, do make enquiries about what is available. In the United Kingdom the 'new' universities are likely to be more innovative in this respect than the 'old', but there are exceptions.

Most institutions set a minimum period of registration for research degrees – usually two years full-time or the equivalent period

---

**Box 2.1**   Recent changes in the provision for postgraduate research in the UK

*Concern to improve submission rates [have] led institutions to introduce new [patterns of research training] ... It is now common for students in the Arts or Social Sciences to undertake a taught element, probably a taught masters degree, before proceeding to a research degree. The ESRC in its 1991 training guidelines required institutions to provide formal taught training programmes for up to 60 per cent of a student's time in the first year of postgraduate study. The Office of Science and Technology initiated a wide-ranging debate over the advantages of a similar taught element for science PhD students. Several forms of MRes (Master of Research)-related courses, which require inter-departmental training ... will be introduced at institutions as pilot projects from October 1995. 'Taught' doctorate degrees are now available .... , and an increasing number of education departments are offering a Doctor of Education degree with combined taught programmes and a significant research element.*
(UK Council for Graduate Education, 1995, p. 8)

---

part-time. In practice, however, it is rare for a PhD to be completed in less than three years. Institutions normally also set a requirement of time 'on campus' and a requirement of attendance at prescribed lectures and courses. These are particularly significant for overseas students wishing to conduct field-work back in their home country.

Routes through a research degree would not be complete without another mention. It is a route appropriate for the mature researcher, who is usually, but not necessarily, well established as a staff member within the institution concerned and who either never went through the normal route for a research degree, or wishes to gain an additional degree. The route is through a collection of books and published, peer-reviewed research articles.

## Making personal contact with the institution

In your own interests, make all your correspondence with an institution as neat and professional-looking as possible. You should apply for admission well before the date you wish to start. Institutions in the United Kingdom normally advise candidates from overseas to apply, if possible, a year in advance, and not to set out from their home countries until they have received and accepted a formal offer.

Prospective research students may be invited to contact a graduate school, where one exists, or to contact departments directly; it is essential to check the instructions in the prospectus. Prospective research students will probably be asked to write a short outline, proposing what they want to do and why, but the precise specification is likely to vary across departments and institutions. Prospective research students whose mother tongue is not English may also be asked to demonstrate competence in the English language (see Box 2.2).

---

**Box 2.2**  Entry requirements for research degree candidates whose mother tongue is not English

Many admissions tutors prefer to assess command of English at interview, but if prospective research students are not available for interview, they may be asked to provide evidence of success in a recognized English language test. The following are indications of the commonly expected minimum scores expected by some institutions. Other institutions may accept less.

International English Language Testing System (IELTS):    7.0
Test of English as a Foreign Language (TOEFL):    550
Associated Examining Board (AEB) Test in English for
    educational purposes:    4

---

## Visiting the institution

You may be invited to see the department; to meet staff, a prospective supervisor and existing research students; and to refine the proposal through discussion. Once there, you will have the opportunity to check the office accommodation and other facilities available to research students and to check whether there are enough research students to make a healthy supportive critical mass. It will be useful to scan Chapter 4 to make a checklist for your enquiries. It is in your best interests to regard the meeting as a two-way interview; you should be interviewing the departmental staff as much as they are interviewing you.

If your visit is in the form of a competitive interview for a research studentship, you will particularly want to impress. Box 2.3 suggests some of the points that the interview panel is likely be looking for in a successful candidate. It will pay you to study them and work on them.

---

**Box 2.3** How to impress at interview for a research studentship

The following is a checklist of what an interview panel is likely to be looking for in the successful candidate:

- ability to grasp concepts and to reason analytically
- motivation and perseverance in achieving objectives
- capacity for independent thought
- organizational skills
- independence as a learner
- self-confidence
- nature and extent of any relevant work experience
- nature and extent of any previously undertaken training in research
- likelihood of establishing a good working relationship with the allocated supervisor and others working in related areas
- language skills, which are particularly important for overseas candidates who have never previously studied in the UK.

(Adapted from Engineering and Physical Sciences Research Council, 1995, p. 5/4)

---

## Writing a proposal for what you want to do

Early on, you will probably be asked to write an outline proposal for what you want to do. What this may involve is likely to vary considerably from one field of study to another. In the arts and humanities, for example, prospective research students will probably be given a free rein on their choice of topic, subject of course to the department's ability to supervise it, and they will have to put in a considerable amount of work in the library to identify and justify it. In science subjects, on the other hand, the research may have to fit in with the availability of expensive equipment provided under a research grant and with what other members of a research group are doing. Then the research topic and the rationale for doing it are provided, and if prospective research students do not like this, or think that appropriate enthusiasm is unlikely to develop, they should apply elsewhere. It is never a good idea to commit oneself to years of something uninspiring, just because of the availability of a place to work on it.

Requirements for an outline proposal differ from department to department, but will probably require the prospective research student to show that the proposed work is worth researching, lends itself to being researched and can be completed within the appropriate time; that it can be adequately resourced; that the prospective research student is suitably qualified to do it; and that no serious constraints exist. The proposal should use language and terminology that is understandable to an intelligent lay person as well as to a subject expert. Most departments, via their admissions tutors or prospective supervisors, do what they can to help prospective research students to make their proposals as clear, detailed and precise as possible. The aim is to provide a safeguard against difficulties arising later, as would be bound to happen if a department were to agree to accept responsibility for a vaguely defined research topic, which subsequently proved difficult to clarify and refine; or if no suitable supervisor could be allocated. This safeguard is unfortunately not foolproof because it requires prospective research students to make decisions about research design before they have necessarily had any training on the subject. The magnitude of this difficulty depends on the field of study, but it is minimized in most cases by general goodwill and professionalism all round. For these and other reasons, the actual research is likely to vary – from somewhat to considerably – from what is in the outline proposal.

In the current climate of rapid change and resource reduction in the United Kingdom, a few departments in a few institutions may not be as careful as they might be about checking that they can provide a research student with what is necessary to carry out the proposed research. It is in your own interests to check for yourself, before registering, that you have found a department that can provide a supervisor, resources and training commensurate with your personal needs and your research topic. If possible, have informal discussions within the department before writing your outline proposal.

## Getting funding

Funding issues are complex, and funding procedures are constantly changing. What follows is intended merely to stimulate your own investigations and your dialogue with institutions. Firstly, check at an early stage the current level of fees in the department of your choice. As a rough guide, in United Kingdom universities, fees for full-time MPhil and PhD students who are citizens of European Union member states will be at least £2000 per year. Part-time fees are likely to be around half of this or less, but this can depend markedly on the institution; overseas students pay about three times the full-time rate; and there may be additional fees in certain heavily resource-dependent subjects. Fees are always under review and likely to change. It will pay not only to check the current position at an institution, but also to shop around.

Getting funding for a research degree is becoming progressively more difficult. Departments may be able to offer bursaries, scholarships, awards, grants or studentships. These may be publicized in some way – sometimes in the national press, through a mailing or via formalized links between individuals, institutions and companies. In the United Kingdom, major sources of funds are the research councils which are accountable to Parliament to ensure that they distribute public research funds to the best possible effect. Candidates for their awards must hold a first or upper second class honours degree in the appropriate field, and even then only a small proportion of those who apply are successful (see Box 2.4). The awards are given only via those departments with completion rates for higher degrees which are deemed satisfactory, and it is to the institutions, not the research councils, that candidates must apply. After interview and/or other procedures, heads of department nominate the individual of their choice for each award.

---

**Box 2.4**    Research council studentships are hard to get!

This extract from the National Postgraduate Committee's *Postgraduate Book* of 1992, although now out of date in terms of the reorganization of the research councils, still makes a hard-hitting point:

*The SERC, the largest research council, turned away 450 applicants with first class degrees. It awarded about 5500 grants, for which it received about 8000 applications ... The British Academy had 3200 applications, 1000 of them with first class degrees, for its 860 grants, while the ESRC can only accept about one sixth of the applications it receives.*
                              (National Postgraduate Committee, 1993, pp. 2–3)

Departments may be able to offer places for collaborative research with industry, research establishments and similar institutions. Registration is normally similar to that for the full-time MPhil and PhD degrees, except that it is subject to an agreement between the institution and the organization where students will work that they will be permitted to conduct the research for a substantial part of their time and that they will be released as appropriate for visits to the institution. The organization, the facilities available and the topic of research must be approved by the head of department prior to registration. A supervisor in the organization concerned is appointed in addition to institutional supervisors.

It is also possible to be paid to do a specified piece of research under a contract which allows the contract researcher to be registered for a research degree in parallel with the contractual work. This provides a helpful source of funding and a ready-made research topic. Before accepting contract research, however, realize that it is not likely to last for the full duration of a PhD degree and that it is normally to produce findings that are in the interests of the provider of the contract, which may not include original work of a PhD standard. So contract researchers, registered for a PhD, usually have to do additional work in their own time.

Many part-time research students will be doing paid outside work, which means that they can either fund themselves, or that they may be able to persuade their employers to fund them, especially where their research and paid work are mutually supportive.

For overseas research students, their government or employer may be able to provide funds to cover full-time fees. If not, for registration within the United Kingdom, the British Council may be able to advise on alternative sources of funding.

It is always worth raising the matter of funding with the admissions tutor in the department where you would like to do your research, just in case there are untapped sources of funding available.

## Using waiting time constructively

Once you receive an offer from an institution, it is only fair to accept or reject it relatively quickly, rather than expect it to be kept open for an indefinite period.

In most institutions, research students can be admitted at any time during the academic year, but the beginning of the academic year in October is best, so as to take advantage of any formal departmental training programmes and any relevant masters courses. This may mean a period of waiting before you actually start – which you should use to advantage. You could, for example, ask the institution to provide background papers, reading lists, registration forms, joining instructions and advice on living accommodation for you to work through. Try to sort out banking arrangements well in advance and suitable living accommodation as soon as possible. Accommodation is considered further in the next chapter.

If you do not already have keyboard skills, acquiring them should be a priority. Quick and accurate typing will be invaluable, irrespective of the type of word processor that you may eventually use once you arrive at the institution. If you can learn on a course, all the better, but there are cheap and effective self-study booklets that can be bought from most booksellers, and you can use them in your own time provided that you have access to a keyboard. Less important, but useful if time permits, is a general familiarity with computers and the most common application packages of word processing, data bases and spreadsheets.

If English it not your first language, you would do well to spend time improving it. Spoken English is as important as written English, and the two are not always developed in tandem. It will be important for you to be able to converse freely, and essential to be understood. So spend time trying to improve your pronunciation as well as your acquisition of new vocabulary. You might try to find a native English speaker to talk to, or failing that, work with audio tapes spoken by a native English speaker.

Finally, many of the suggestions in this book require elapsed thinking time, an incubation period, to generate the greatest benefit. So it would be a good use of time to peruse the book now, while waiting to enrol. In particular, Chapters 3, 5, 15 and 16 will repay early attention.

# 3 PREPARING FOR THE WAY OF LIFE OF A RESEARCH STUDENT

*To be forewarned is to be forearmed.*

(Proverb)

## The importance of recognizing the need for adjustment

Being a research student has to be a way of life, not just a job, because it cannot simply be locked away into whatever is done inside the institution during office hours. The implications are different for everyone. Everyone has a unique personal background, expectations, needs and responsibilities to others; and everyone carries assumptions about how they expect to live their lives.

It is important to think about the implications of personal circumstances as early as possible, preferably before going ahead with the decision to become a research student, and certainly before arrival in the institution. Research degrees, unlike degrees at undergraduate or masters level, are seldom failed. They are simply not completed – research students let their work fade out to the extent that it is too difficult to pick up again. Causes nearly always lie with personal circumstances.

This chapter flags up some of the more common personal circumstances that can adversely affect the efficient and effective conduct of the work and lives of research students. The aim is to forewarn you at an early stage, so that you can head them off and prevent them from ever becoming significant. Later chapters consider them more fully.

(■)  **Activity**

Tick all the circumstances in the following checklist which apply or will apply to you.

- Full-time
- Part-time
- Mature student
- Employed in an outside job
- Recently graduated from first degree
- English not first language
- From overseas
- Living with parents
- Living with a partner
- Caring for children
- Caring for aged relatives
- Living at home
- Living away from home
- Living with other research students
- Spending several hours in travel in from home or base
- Finances likely to be a problem

Now add any other of your personal circumstances which may possibly have an influence on your life as a research student.

(■)  **Discussion of activity**

Of all the differences in the personal circumstances of research students, that with most implications is probably whether they are part- or full-time. Part-timers are almost always mature (that is, not straight from their first degree), whereas full-timers may or may not be. Often they are earning their living within a career which takes much of their time and makes it difficult to block out time for research or to attend seminars and relevant masters courses. Often part-timers live at home and have personal and financial responsibilities to their families. Although some of these personal circumstances exist for full-timers too, full-timers certainly have more uninterrupted time for their work. Useful advice for part-time students is referenced in the Further Reading section.

Overseas students usually have additional personal circumstances which have implications for their work. Irrespective of whether they are living with their immediate families, they are certainly separated from the security of the traditions, customs and support of their home communities. Some may also have to cope with the language of their studies, English, being foreign.

The following sections consider some of these issues, to prepare you for what might lie ahead.                                     ●

## Living at home versus having other accommodation

Research students who live away from home need to find accommodation that is convenient and congenial. The institution may have its own accommodation on or close to campus, and there should be an accommodation office to advise on seeking private rented accommodation and tenancy agreements. Once in some sort of accommodation, a good way to find something better is to take advantage of informal networks to hear about accommodation about to be vacated.

Some research students are lonely at first. If you think that loneliness may affect you, reserve a definite small portion of time for socializing. In the long run, it will support and not detract from progress with your research degree. This is a continuing theme throughout the book, but especially of Chapters 11 and 17.

Living at home is comfortable and companionable, but skills and strategies have to be developed to cope with the distractions there and to keep those members of the family happy who may feel that they have a right to more of your time. Chapters 11 and 17 offer suggestions. There is a related issue about which this book can do no more than forewarn. It is that research students living with non-academic partners need to be sensitive to any signs that their partners are feeling threatened or 'left behind' at not being able to keep up academically. The likelihood and significance of this cannot be over-emphasized, and the fact that problems tend not to surface until some time into the programme of study can produce a false sense of security early on.

Living with other research students has advantages and disadvantages. The advantages are the benefits of interacting with them; the disadvantages are being distracted from work. Chapters 9 and 11 respectively offer strategies for combating the latter and enhancing the former.

## English as a mother tongue versus English as a foreign language

Research students who have English as a mother tongue have a head start on those who do not. The English for academic reading and writing of most such research students tends to be good. However, spoken English is also important. One reason concerns the benefits of being able to communicate freely and easily with supervisors and other research students. Another is that some institutions regard their PhD as implying possession of the skills to discuss, argue and possibly later also to teach in English. As far as language skills are concerned, the problem for overseas students in the United Kingdom is that they tend to conduct their social lives with people from their own countries, so that they can relax in their own culture and interact without language difficulties. Whereas this is entirely understandable, it does nothing to develop spoken English. So, if English is not your mother tongue, do make an effort from early on to take opportunities to include native English speakers in your social life.

## Home cultures versus Western culture

All cultures invariably give respect where respect is due, but ways of demonstrating this respect vary across cultures. In particular, some cultures expect a student never to stray from giving the outward appearance that a teacher is right in all respects all of the time. These cultures value deference, humility and compliance, with no displays of emotion. Research students from such cultures face a major readjustment when they first arrive in a Western university where independent thinking is valued and where research students are expected to demonstrate this in ways which may seem alien and uncomfortable.

Some supervisors are sensitive to these issues and help their research students handle them, but supervisors who have never worked in different cultures may not be. This puts the onus on the research students. The issues will not go away, and unless they are sorted out, the path to the research degree will be strewn with difficulties. Remedies are matters for individual preference, often worked out with guidance from more experienced members of the same culture.

Often all that is needed is a form of 'permission' from supervisors that academic argument and creative thinking are acceptable within the research degree framework; that this is what will in fact give supervisors satisfaction; and that it will not be regarded as lack of respect. Chapter 6 suggests ways of taking initiatives with supervisors on this and various other matters.

Research students from non-Western cultures also need to understand that supervisors, just like everyone else, can be sufficiently insecure to feel threatened in certain situations. Some ways of handling this are also given in Chapter 6.

## Living close to the institution versus spending hours in travel

The advantages of living near one's place of work are self-evident: travel is cheaper and less tiring, and social events can more easily be attended in the evenings. If you have to travel long distances, try to do it at a time when you can get a seat, and use the time to read, work on a portable computer or talk with fellow-travelling research students.

If you live a long way from the institution, you need contingency plans for seminars or supervisions being cancelled at short notice when you have already travelled in for them. Such plans are part of time management skills and are considered in Chapter 9.

## Self-financed versus being on a grant

The method by which research students are financed can have a very strong bearing on the progress of their studies. Research students funded by outside agencies have to make an exceptionally good case if they are to have their grants extended to give extra time to complete. This means that such students have to settle down quickly to the business of getting the research degree. Self-funded students have more freedom to pursue research at a more leisurely pace – although all United Kingdom universities are under pressure to speed up completion rates. Deeply scholastic theses, taking many years to complete, are generally a thing of the past.

Box 3.1 gives some ideas for making money go further. Although most of them are obvious, they may nevertheless have slipped your mind and be worth implementing early on.

**Box 3.1**   What to do when the money runs out

- State handouts. There are not many left! If you are a UK citizen, it is worth getting an AG1 form from an optician, dentist or DSS office. You may well get free prescriptions, eye tests and dental checkups if eligible. This form is designed to put people off. Fill it in; it could save you a lot of money.
- Watch those transport costs. If you travel by public transport, don't just assume that buying a travel card/season ticket is the cheapest option. Often it is not if you don't have to come in every day. Don't forget that a bicycle or walking is the cheapest form of transport.
- Don't live at the Ritz. It is always worth looking to see if you can move somewhere cheaper or nearer. Halls of residence are often cheap, if you can get a place. The most important advice is to seek help from the institution's accommodation office. Finally, living with relatives may be unbearable, but it can be cheap!
- If you can get some kind of job, it will help your situation considerably. It is worth visiting the careers service on a regular basis. If you have any special talents, this is a good time to discover them.
- Shopping for bargains. Supermarket own brand items are often considerably cheaper than branded products and often just as good. Try markets and second-hand shops for clothes and CDs.
- Managing your money. Don't put £2000 under the bed. Don't put it in a student bank account either. Put it into a high-interest building society account or (if you are brave) a unit trust (they can go down as well as up). Use credit cards to buy items like books and travel cards. Pay when you get a statement; under no circumstances pay any interest charges. Remember that heating bills are related to how much you use your heating!
- Be nice to people. You may wonder what this has to do with finance. However, it is very important – especially with parents or spouses. If you want people to support you or make sacrifices for you, you need to be nice to them. Remember birthdays (particularly your mother's) and make people think that you appreciate their help. That way they are likely to go out of their way to help you. Bank managers also appreciate being told that you want to go into overdraft before you do.
- Do they do a student discount? A surprisingly large number of places do. Don't be afraid to ask – many places do not advertise

the fact. It is also worth using any money-saving vouchers you can get your hands on. If you have not got an NUS card, it is worth getting one for discounts.

- Selling the family silver. Many people plead poverty but appear wealthy. Each of us has various bits and pieces we keep in a cupboard somewhere. Books are especially prone to sitting idly on bookshelves. Remember that second-hand bookshops buy as well as sell. Virtually everything can be sold for a price.

(Adapted from University College London Graduate School, 1994, p. 4)

*NB.* Issue 2 of the University College *Graduate Society Newsletter* elicited responses from staff which flagged up the existence of hardship and travel funds of which postgraduates could take advantage. These were specific to University College London, but suggest that it would be worth finding out what other institutions can offer.

## Other personal circumstances

You may have – or imagine that you have – special circumstances which could affect your being taken seriously or fully accepted in the new academic community. You could, for example, be considerably older than the average research student and think that you could be a target for ageism; or you could be from a background that makes you think that you could be the target of sexism. There are many other such '-isms', and all sorts of terms could be coined for what is imagined to cause or genuinely does cause prejudice in others. Although genuine and deep-rooted prejudice does exist, most of it is either imagined or can be negated over time by appropriate professional behaviour. If you think that an '-ism' is likely to bother you, make resolutions to get advice from others who seem to be coping well with the same 'handicap', and to set up or join self-help support groups on campus. These groups can be as large or small, formal or informal, transient or ongoing, as you and other members find appropriate for your own needs.

This book is not the place to advise on what to do if other personal difficulties arise. Use your judgement about how far to load supervisors with personal matters. Most institutions provide alternative sources of help (see Chapter 4).

⬛  **Activity**

---

If you think that you need study skills or work strategies to meet
any other special circumstances in which you find yourself, make a
note of the problems here. Then ask around for suggestions.

---

# 4 SETTLING IN AS A NEW RESEARCH STUDENT

*We were forming a group of people who'd be working together and learning together, going through similar experiences, creating together. I thought it was terrific.*
(Leonard Nimoy, quoted in Shatner, 1993, p. 204)

## The importance of being a fully integrated member of the department or research group

Once you arrive in the department or group where you are to do your research, the sooner you can settle in, the sooner you can start productive work. This chapter is about speeding up the settling-in process. It involves finding out about the facilities and people there to support you, familiarizing yourself with them and then putting yourself in a position to take advantage of them.

## Responsibilities for your integration

A department or group with a large number of research students enrolling at the same time, probably at the beginning of the academic year, will probably run formal induction events and supply folders of useful information. Much of the responsibility for integrating yourself will thus be taken off you, and you will have little need of this chapter, although it is probably worth scanning quickly.

There may, however, be few if any formal procedures for induction, perhaps because the department or group is small, or because you are enrolling at a time other than the beginning of the academic year. In this case, you have to take responsibility for your own integration. This chapter provides a stimulus for action, but it can do no more than that because departments and groups are so different in terms of the resources at their disposal, their management preferences, and the needs and requirements of their disparate disciplines.

If you are part-time, this chapter is particularly for you. It is all too easy to assume that shortage of time will necessarily prevent you from availing yourself of all but the most basic of what the department or group can offer. Although it is true that the calls on your time will be severe and that you will have to identify priorities, this does not mean that you should allow decisions to be made and behaviour patterns to develop by default through lack of information.

## Familiarizing yourself with departmental accommodation

With the best will in the world, departments vary enormously in terms of what accommodation their resources allow them to provide for their research students. The extract in Box 4.1 by a former officer of a postgraduate student union is part of an article which is well worth reading in full. It gives the results of one analysis of needs, and many departments manage to achieve its recommendations for their full-time research students. It may be beyond their means to do the same for part-timers, although it is reasonable that part-timers should at least have somewhere to put their coats and books, if they are to stay longer in the department than merely popping in to see their supervisors and then leaving again, and that

---

**Box 4.1**   Space and facilities for research students

*Accommodation of research students must be specialised to meet three ends. First, every research student must have an office, possibly shared, to be used as 'home base'. This will have to include certain other facilities. Second, students sharing offices will require part-time exclusive access to other departmental rooms. Third, each department above a certain size needs a common room set aside for its research students only. Common space is a valuable weapon in the war against isolation.*

*Each student needs a place of his/her own. The minimum acceptable provision is a desk, chair, lamp, bookcase, file drawer(s), telephone and room key. . . .*

(Gross, 1994, p. 21)

they should have adequate laboratory space and workshop space where appropriate.

Use the activity as a stimulus for finding out what departmental accommodation is available for research students. If you are asking questions outside a formal induction programme, use your judgement about who to approach, depending on who seems knowledgeable and prepared to chat. Some possibilities are supervisors, other research students, the departmental secretary, and the member of staff with special responsibility for research students where one exists. Everyone is bound to be busy. Social occasions, such as coffee or lunch breaks, when people seem happy to talk, are a norm in some departments, but unheard of in others.

(■)   **Activity**

What does the department provide for its research students in the way of the following?

• An office to work in

• A desk

• A locker for bags

• Somewhere to hang clothes

• Coffee-making facilities

• Laboratory and workshop space, where appropriate

• Any other accommodation

How, if at all, is the accommodation different for full-timers and part-timers?

**Discussion of activity**

The extract in Box 4.2 gives a flavour of the importance of adequate office space for research students.

---

**Box 4.2**   The importance of proper accommodation for research students

*The provision of better office space for all research students will have major and longlasting benefits for all interested parties. Students will be better able to proceed with their work and will feel more satisfied by their postgraduate experience. Members of staff will find that creating a cohesive body of research students will give them a readily available body of help for research, teaching, seminars and other activities. The community will be enhanced by the inclusion of its senior students. The funding bodies will also approve.*

(Gross, 1994, p. 24)

---

## Familiarizing yourself with departmental facilities and services

Departments also vary in terms of what general facilities and services they can provide for their research students. Use the activity as a stimulus for finding out about them.

    **Activity**

---

Find out the procedures for research students:

• Collecting incoming mail


• Using a phone for incoming calls


Procedures for the following may not be available and, if they are, they may not be free. Find out what they are, how any payment works and whether, where appropriate, similar facilities may be used more cheaply nearby.

• A phone for outgoing calls

• A photocopier

• A fax machine

• Departmental stationery

• Departmental computers, printers and application packages

• Specially produced in-house software

• E-mail, for sending and receiving messages electronically

• Other Internet services such as World Wide Web, File Transfer Protocol, Gopher, etc.

• Keys to research students' work areas

If you do not already own a computer, is it worth getting one? If so:

• What type of computer would make you compatible with supervisors and/or others in the department?

• What application packages (word processing, data bases, spreadsheets, etc.) would you need to make you compatible with others in the department?

• How can your own computer be made to communicate with those in the department?

(■)  **Discussion of activity**

A perennial problem for research students is the cost of facilities. Clearly it is in your best interests to try to get what you can as cheaply as you can. It is part of research training to learn to work within a budget.                                                                  (■)

## Familiarizing yourself with the system of supervisory support

There may be various systems of supervisory support in operation. Where a supervisor has not yet supervised a doctoral research student through to completion, many institutions require there to be an experienced formal supervisor, who keeps a watchful eye on the supervision process. In those 'new' universities which are still developing their research tradition, the formal supervisor may be overseeing a number of research students and new supervisors, and may have a formal role which is often known as 'Director of Studies'.

Where a research topic is known from the outset to require the expertise of more than one individual, research students may start with joint supervisors or even a team, panel or committee of supervisors, each having a particular role or responsibility. Sometimes the need for joint supervisors emerges over time as unforeseen avenues open up; then additional supervisors may be appointed. There may also be external supervisors from other institutions. Use the activity below to find out what is available.

Some departments provide their research students with mentors or advisers, who are members of academic staff other than the formal supervisors, to whom a student can turn for impartial advice and support.

Another common practice is for there to be a single member of staff with general responsibility for the research students in the department. Such an individual is likely to have an interest in research; to sit on a research committee of the institution; to be the intermediary between the Registry and research students; and to be responsible for any formalized group training. His or her role could be both administrative and pastoral. Alternatively, the role may be shared across a department or institution by members of a committee.

Your task now is to find out what systems of supervisory support are available to you. The pros and cons of seeking or managing multi-supervision are considered later in Chapter 6.

(■)  **Activity**

---

Find out the names and roles of everyone who has a formal supervisory responsibility towards you, for example:

- The single person, probably just called your supervisor, who undertakes day-to-day supervision.* This is someone you will almost certainly have already met.

- A principal supervisor, who oversees supervision, but does not have a day-to-day involvement.

- A team, panel or committee of supervisors, with a joint responsibility or with each member having a unique responsibility.

- Joint supervisors, with equal responsibility towards you, but in different areas of your work.

- A collaborative supervisor, who supervises from the perspective of an outside organization or agency.

- A mentor or adviser.

- Anyone else, such as a visiting expert of some sort.

---

(■)  **Discussion of activity**

The rest of the book would make clumsy reading if it kept using a form of words to encompass all the possibilities of supervisory

---

* The term 'day-to-day' applied to a supervisor and to supervision implies 'first-port-of-call'. Although in some departments the possibility for casual meetings may be there on a day-to-day basis, no implication is intended that meetings should of necessity take place every day.

support. So, unless stated otherwise, the single term 'supervisor' will be used for the individual staff member who has day-to-day responsibility for you. Where you have additional supervisory support, you will need to adapt the terminology for your own circumstances.    ⬤

## Familiarizing yourself with departmental research training and support

Departments vary in terms of what general training and support they provide for research students. Use the activity below as a stimulus for finding out what is available for you.

⬤  **Activity**

---

Apart from the interaction between research students and their supervisors, is any general training offered? If so what is its form?

• An induction programme

• Weekly (or other regular) seminars

• Relevant masters courses to sit in on

• Other courses to sit in on

• Some form of group support

Are there any social events which bring staff and research students together?

Where can copies of course materials and reprints of research articles be obtained?

If there is a graduate school, does it offer any training and support in addition to that of the department?

---

(■)   **Discussion of activity**

Training programmes can be essential, helpful or wastefully time-consuming, depending on their scope and the background and needs of research students. In particular, there is the inevitable conflict between the need to start the research as soon as possible and the need to find out about research design and research methods so as not to waste time on what may turn out to be inappropriate. You must clearly do as much of both as is reasonable. Your supervisor's advice is crucial in establishing what is reasonable for you.   (■)

## Familiarizing yourself with departmental staff and research groups

Each member of academic staff in the department will have his or her own personal area of research, possibly with a group of research officers, research assistants and research students working in various aspects of that area. The research areas of some staff may be so closely related that they and their students together form a research group, which may or may not extend outside the department.

It is also important to find out about the other departmental staff: the secretaries, the administrators, the post-doctoral researchers and, in some fields of study, the technical staff. You will need their confidence and friendship.

Use the activity on the following page as a stimulus for finding out about staff and research groups in the department.

⬛ **Activity**

What are the areas of research in the department and who heads them?

Where, if at all, do all the other academic and research staff within the department fit into these research areas?

If you are to be part of a research group in which one or more research students work on parts of a single large topic, what, in general terms, are the boundaries of the work of each of you? Or what will be the procedures for identifying them as the work develops?

Do any research groups have activities which it might be worth keeping informed about or being involved in?

What links are there between research groups?

What are the areas of responsibility of the secretarial, administrative and, where appropriate, library and technical staff in the department?

Do they ask that research students follow any particular procedures when requesting their services?

## Familiarizing yourself with departmental and institutional procedures

Every department and institution has its own way of doing things. Some of this will be documented as formal procedures, although much will be implicit and undocumented. It is too easy to become drowned in unnecessary paper, so seek guidance about what documents are worth having and when. Use the activity below as a checklist.

### (■)  Activity

Are there documented departmental or institutional procedures on any of the following?

• Study contracts for research students


• Notes of guidance for research students


• Roles and responsibilities of supervisors and research students

- Procedures for monitoring research students' progress and, in particular, for transferring from MPhil to PhD

- Health and safety regulations, where appropriate for the field of study

What other useful or important documents exist for research students, and at what stage is it worth studying them?

---

(■)   **Discussion of activity**

Some departments operate a form of learning contract which documents the results of negotiations with the department, possibly via the supervisor, on a number of points. The process of negotiation and ultimate agreement constitutes a sound basis for understanding what is required of you and what research students have a right to expect.                                                              (■)

## Familiarizing yourself with institutional and other libraries

All institutions of higher education have a library or libraries, often with a number of librarians who specialize in particular disciplines. If such individuals exist in your library, for your field of study, you would be well advised to cultivate their acquaintance. They can be of real help during your research programme.

There may be nearby libraries which are open to members of your institution, and there may also be specialist libraries elsewhere which you can arrange to use, possibly on payment of a fee. Your supervisor, other research students or the institutional library should be able to provide the necessary information.

Do not ignore public libraries; they may provide loan copies more cheaply and quickly than institutional libraries.

⬛ **Activity**

---

How do research students get a library card?

Are there enough desks for working in the library, and how quiet is it?

How does one find out about the facilities that the library offers?

If there is a librarian specializing in your field of study, who is he or she?

What other libraries might it be worth using and how does one go about doing so?

---

## Locating other institutional facilities and services

Of the other institutional facilities and services, the most urgent to find out about is the health centre and how, if necessary, to register with a local doctor. Next in urgency, if you are an overseas student, is to find out what institutional support exists for you – perhaps a language centre to help with written and spoken English and/or a social club.

Institutions normally have a wide range of other facilities and services, such as: a students' union; computing services; print services; counselling services; financial services; services to help with language problems; chaplaincies for major religions; accommodation services; careers services; shops; eating places; etc. Some even have a research students' support group and a nursery for young children of research students. These facilities and services are probably best investigated as you need them.

## Identifying useful national organizations

There are national organizations which exist to support and/or to develop policies for postgraduate research students, and it would be useful, in due course, to familiarize yourself with their remits. Within the United Kingdom the following are particularly worth noting:

- The National Postgraduate Committee was formed in 1982 to represent the interests and aspirations of all postgraduates whether on taught courses or undertaking research. It keeps some records on national subject networks, and it may be worth making contact to see if there is a postgraduate network for your subject area.
- The United Kingdom Council for Graduate Education was established in 1994 to promote a distinct identity for graduate education and research in higher education.
- The Council for International Education gives advice to institutions and students on matters relating to overseas students. It is still known as UKCOSA which stood for its old name, United Kingdom Council for Overseas Students' Affairs.

Addresses are at the end of the book.

The best support may come from the postgraduate section, if one exists, of the learned or professional society for your field of study.

(■) **Activity**

---

Find out, possibly by enquiring of your supervisor, other staff in the department or the library, whether there is a learned or professional society for your field of study, and if so what its address is.

Take advice within the department and, if it seems appropriate, make contact with the society to see if it has a postgraduate section and what support that can provide.

---

⬛  **Discussion of activity**

Research tends to be an individual activity, and as a programme of research progresses, a major complaint from research students is likely to be a feeling of isolation. Unless you are working on a group project or as part of a large and active research department, you should put effort into warding off isolation. You need to be on the constant lookout for people who both know enough about your field to be able to discuss it meaningfully and have the time to do so. You may find such people in your family, in your social group or in your department; visiting staff on sabbatical leave are ideal. However, if you have to go outside into a national or international arena, so be it. Overcoming isolation or potential isolation must be a major objective for all research students.    ⬛

# 5 TOWARDS RECOGNIZING GOOD RESEARCH

*A PhD from a UK university is widely (if not universally) admired in terms of its quality.*

(Clark, 1995)

## The importance of recognizing good research

Although high standards in research build on the academic excellence that should already have been acquired from undergraduate or taught masters work, more is involved – as those research students who have experienced supervised projects or dissertations will appreciate. Some departments ease research students gently in by giving them rigorous supervision on a small pilot project. This has the advantage of providing the experience of the totality of research, from the design stage right through to writing up, and therefore gives a feel for what lies ahead with the real thing. It helps research students to monitor their own progress and accordingly saves time and frustration later. Some departments may feel, on the other hand, that time is too short for anything which detracts from the main work.

This chapter is for research students who do not have the advantage of a thoroughly supervised pilot project. The purpose is to give a feel for the things that contribute to good research – but it is only a beginning of a journey which never entirely ends. The chapter is a guided study of research articles and theses. If you think you would benefit from working through it, ask your supervisor or other research students to recommend some ten or so research articles that are respected in your area, together with a couple of MPhil theses and a few PhD theses. Theses, being so long, can be time-consuming to wade through; so the research articles will tend to demonstrate some points more readily. Incidentally, libraries do not allow theses or journals to be taken out of the building, but they can be studied on site. Alternatively, supervisors may be prepared to lend personal copies.

Before looking at the articles and theses, a word of warning. Each field of study has its own norms, informed through experience of dealing with similar types of research. An idea of the extent of the differences is given in Box 5.1. There is thus no way that this chapter can give specific guidance that is acceptable for all fields of study. Nevertheless, the general guidance should be useful as a starting point for discussion among members of your discipline.

---

**Box 5.1**    Postgraduate research is different in different disciplines

*In science, research education is strongly shaped by the conditions required for maximising the productivity of specialised research groups. Students are recruited to a research group geared towards defining discrete sets of problems. Students will undoubtedly contribute to their solution. But sometimes the needs of the research are difficult to combine with those of the student. It might, for example, be in a highly competitive and rapidly changing field where speed is of the essence. . . . Students' contribution to the work of their group may often be substantial. But their contribution to disciplinary knowledge is normally predefined by their supervisor and expectations of originality are limited.*

*. . . In the humanities the traditional emphasis has been on individual modes of inquiry and on the importance of the freedom of the student to select his or her research topic. Originality and independence are strongly held values . . . Claims of substantial contributions to knowledge on the part of PhD students are still made, but only from the most prestigious institutions.*

*. . . In the social sciences . . . the ideal remains that of the individual pursuing the problem of his or her choice and making a more or less original contribution. Concepts of originality are usually but not always fairly modest . . .*

(Becher *et al.*, 1995, pp. 13–14)

---

## Research topics and problems

Research students normally start their work with a general area of interest, which may or may not have been provided for them by a supervisor or research group. At some stage this may be expressed as a precise problem to be solved by investigation. However, the stage at which this is done varies widely.

At one extreme the research problem is specified as soon into the research as possible. It tends to be presented as a set of research questions or hypotheses that grow out of the general area or topic. Care and attention are given to make these so detailed and specific that decisions about how to go about getting the appropriate data become straightforward, being little more than a process of rewording. Large portions and possibly all of the research design thus fall naturally into place. With this approach, getting the research questions and hypotheses into a form which has the right amount of detail is a crucial early part of the whole research undertaking. (The process is known as 'operationalizing' the research questions and hypotheses.)

At the other extreme, the wording of the research problem, as given in the thesis, tends to be finalized towards the end of the work, as understanding grows. Each step of the research takes up and explores interesting or significant parts of what emerged from previous steps, and as the significant foci reveal themselves, they form the basis of the research problem as it is finally elucidated.

The usual approach to defining a research problem is to read round the subject to get to know the background and to identify unanswered questions or controversies, and/or to conduct small-scale investigations or pilot studies to identify the most significant issues for further exploration. The relative balance between these varies according to the nature of the work and accordingly from one field of study to another.

The following activity invites you to get a feel for how research topics or problems tend to be identified in your field of study. It cannot be emphasized enough that the purpose is to raise issues to discuss further with your supervisor and other research students. Make sure that you do so, and do not be surprised if they feel that both the terminology and the questions need considerable modification to be applicable for your field of study.

● **Activity**

Scan the PhD theses in your sample. (Do not attempt to read them in full.) Is it usual in your field to define the research problem in terms of a list of specific research questions or hypotheses? Alter-

LIBRARY
EDUCATION CENTRE
PRINCESS ROYAL HOSPITAL

natively, does it seem usual for the focus or foci of the research topic
to emerge as the work progresses?

Is there any indication in the theses that the actual research problem or topic changed dramatically or in emphasis during the period
of the research?

If a research problem was formulated early on in terms of research
questions and hypotheses, how well do these lead naturally and
easily to decisions about how the research needed to be designed?

---

## Research methodologies

A rationale for the methods used to gather and process data, in what
sequence and on what samples, taken together, constitutes a research methodology. This is not a grand term for 'list of methods',
but an informed argument for designing research in a particular
way. A research methodology needs to be appropriate for the research problem, and the justification that this is so should form part
of a thesis. Box 5.2 gives some definitions of 'methodology' quite
generally. The suffix '-ology' means 'the study of'; hence the terms
sociology, psychology, etc.

---

**Box 5.2**   Some dictionary definitions of 'methodology'

*The science of method.*

*(Shorter Oxford English Dictionary)*

*A body of methods, procedures, working concepts, rules and
postulates.*

*(Webster's International Unabridged Dictionary)*

---

It takes experience of research in the discipline concerned to comment on the appropriateness of a research methodology for a particular research problem, but you should be able to see how well methodologies are argued for in the theses and how reasonable they seem in the articles.

(■) **Activity**

How well do you feel that the research methodologies in the articles and theses are argued for?

## Research competence

Once the investigations have been carried out, data of some sort should have accumulated. Data* needs to be as relevant and accurate as possible for several reasons. One reason is to inspire confidence in the eventual solution to the research problem. The extract in Box 5.3 is about the criticisms that careless researchers can lay

---

**Box 5.3** The importance of data being relevant

Hans Eysenck has the following to say of the psychologist Cyril Burt:

*Burt, while outstanding in his ability to use statistical methods in the analysis of data relating to intellectual or personality differences, was rather careless about the quality of the data he analysed. As I once told him: 'You use the most advanced methods of psychometrics in your analyses, but you use them on data that are quite dubious – tests done unsupervised by teachers, for instance . . . .' This did not increase his liking for me . . .*
(Eysenck, 1994)

---

* In line with modern and idiomatic usage, this book takes 'data' as a collective singular noun.

themselves open to in this connection. Another reason is that sometimes something unexpected turns up which can lead to an entirely new and important line of investigation. Before pursuing this line, however, the researcher needs to be fairly confident that the anomaly is not just 'noise in the system'. The anecdote in Box 5.4 is about a careful and competent researcher who was able to have just such confidence. A third reason is that constraints of time, location or availability of source material often prevent a data collection exercise from being repeated as a check.

---

**Box 5.4**   The importance of data being untainted

The British astronomy research student Joscelyn Bell Burnell noticed scuffs on photographic plates of the night sky which she was routinely surveying. Since she had confidence in how well she was keeping the plates, she knew that the scuffs could not just be dirt or stray light. So she investigated them further and as a result 'pulsars' were discovered. On the basis of this, a Nobel prize was awarded to her supervisor Antony Hewish and his colleague. She went on to become a professor of physics at the Open University.

---

(■)   **Activity**

---

Scan the theses and articles. To what extent do they convince you that the investigations concerned were competently conducted?

---

## Academic argument and academic discourse

Probably one of the most important things to learn about good research is that theses and research articles should be much more than reports on work carried out. They need to be arguments, counter-arguments and reflection – on such matters as how the research problem was identified; how it was investigated; what data was obtained; what the outcomes were and their importance. In essence, a thesis should be a documented case for solution(s) to research problem(s).

Arguments need to be written in the language of academic discourse of the subject, with each word having a precise meaning. Arguments need to be substantiated throughout with primary data (data collected by the researcher) and secondary data (facts, findings, etc. processed and discussed by others). These must be clearly distinguished from each other. Arguments should not be blurred with irrelevances, and counter-arguments must be openly acknowledged and dealt with rigorously and fairly.

---

**Box 5.5**   Argument, counter-argument and reflection

*To travel illuminatingly is more important than to arrive . . . The route must take in all the most interesting points and yet maintain an overall sense of direction.*

(Pirie, 1991, p. 53)

---

 **Activity**

---

• For each research article, summarize what its argument is.

• Now try to identify some arguments in the theses. This will take longer and you will probably not think it worth the time to carry on to completion, because theses are large documents and will probably have a number of intertwined streams of argument. The places to scan for the form of the arguments are the abstract, preface, introduction or overview (whatever is the norm in the subject area); the contents list; the first and last paragraphs of each chapter; and the final chapter.

• To what extent do you feel that the theses in your sample have cogent arguments? Do you feel anywhere that the arguments are blurred with 'padding'?

• To what extent do you feel that the theses in your sample acknowledge and deal fairly with counter-arguments?

• In terms of quality of argument and academic discourse, are there any notable differences between the MPhil and the PhD theses?

---

### (■)  Discussion of activity

All the theses in the sample should be logically and coherently argued, but some will inevitably be better argued than others. (Research degrees are not normally graded.) You may feel that the PhD theses are more soundly argued than the MPhil ones. Certainly inability to argue is one reason, but only one, why research students are not permitted to upgrade from MPhil to PhD, or to pass through whatever other probationary barrier is currently in operation.  (■)

## Outcomes of research

Solutions to research problems may be the culmination of any piece of research. There may, however, be other outcomes, and these are often so important that the thesis is written entirely with hindsight to make these additional or unexpected outcomes a focus of the research problem. So changes of direction may not be immediately clear from a thesis.

It is worth looking at a range of possible outcomes from research at PhD level because it will stimulate you, in due course, to be more creative in the formulation or later reformulation of your own research topic or problem, and to recognize the significance of the unexpected when it arises in your own work. So use the following activity to see what sorts of outcome seem to be usual in your field.

(■)   **Activity**

On the basis of the articles and theses in your sample, what types of solution to research problems or other types of outcome seem to be usual?

Talk to research students who are near completion to see what types of solution or outcome they are anticipating.

Check your conclusions about possible and usual types of solution or outcome by discussing them with your supervisor and members of your department or group.

## ◼ Discussion of activity

Outcomes of research and solutions to research problems are wide-ranging in nature. Take a look at the extract in Box 5.6, which is used to stimulate thinking in workshops for research students. Although some of the examples may be abstract, others are tangible, and this illustrates that there is no significant difference in the processes known as research, research and development, and research and design. How much development or design can be included in a thesis depends on the field of study and the institutional regulations.

---

**Box 5.6**   Some possible solutions to research problems and outcomes of postgraduate research: a checklist to stimulate thinking

- *A new product. There are many examples in all fields of study. Products which were once original and can readily be appreciated as such by lay persons might include: a book, a synthetic fabric, a synthetic food.*
- *A development of or an improvement on something which already exists. There is a hazy borderline between a new product and an improvement on an existing one. For example, can a design of a five-bedroom house be new in itself or can it only be a development of a design for a two-bedroom house?*
- *A new theory. Well-known examples of what were once new theories are Darwin's theory of evolution and the Big Bang theory for the origins of the universe.*
- *A reinterpretation of an existing theory. There is a hazy borderline between a new theory and a reinterpretation of an existing one. An example might be how the absence of certain fossils in the fossil record forces Darwin's theory of evolution to be reappraised.*
- *A new research tool or technique. An example might be a computer package to undertake certain tasks; a piece of equipment to identify heart defects; or a set of questionnaires to identify problem areas in certain sections of the community.*
- *A new model or perspective. All fields of study can be looked at in a new way. An example from science fiction would be the perspective of thinking of time as a fourth dimension, which can be travelled through, like the other dimensions of length, breadth and height.*

---

- *An in-depth study. In all fields of study there can be the
  opportunity to study something that has never been studied
  before, such as, the moons of Jupiter, following the enormous
  amount of data collected by the Galileo probe, or the Van
  Gogh painting which was thought to be lost and has recently
  been rediscovered.*
- *A critical analysis. Examples might be an analysis of a novel or
  of the effects of a government or economic policy.*
- *A portfolio of work based on research. Professionals in many
  fields can produce these.*
- *A collection of generalizable findings or conclusions. This is a
  particularly common outcome of research in all fields. An
  example might be factors which favour or militate against crime
  on housing estates.*
- *Something else. There are always examples of other outcomes
  of research.*

(Author's workshop handout)

## Documentation of literature

Properly written-up research should cite literature in a consistent
manner according to the norms of the discipline. Three methods are
in common use:

- References are indicated in the text by the author's surname and
  the year of publication; and the sources are collected together at
  the end of the thesis presented in alphabetical order of authors.
- References are numbered consecutively in the text and the sources
  are collected together at the end of the thesis in the order cited.
  (All good word processors take care of the renumbering automatically when another reference is added mid-text.)
- References are given as footnotes on the page where they appear,
  denoted by a symbol or number. (Again, good word processors
  take care of this automatically.)

Research students should already be familiar with normal practice
in their discipline for listing references. However, most research students need to remind themselves of the details for the various types
of publication. Use the following activity as an *aide-mémoire*.

⬛ **Activity**

How is a publication referred to within the text of the articles and theses in your sample?

What information is given, and in what order, about each of the following in the reference section of an article or thesis?

- A book written by a single author

- A book written by several authors

- A book of contributions from several authors

- A journal article

- A conference paper

- A thesis

- Any other document that is part of the literature of your subject, for example a government publication or a law report, including any that do not give an author

If any of the abbreviations in references are new to you, list them.

⬛ **Discussion of activity**

Note, in particular, that full references require page numbers. It is all too easy to forget to note them when examining a text; and it can be very time-consuming and irritating to have to find them out again later.

For advice on referencing, see the recommendations in the Further Reading section.

## Use of literature

Ideally literature should be used in articles and theses as evidence to support an argument or counter-argument or to carry it forward. The absence of literature can be used in the same way, provided that this is convincing and not a ploy for inadequate literature surveys.

In theses, literature should additionally be used to show a thorough knowledge of the field. This can involve a fine balancing act between lists and arguments, because mere entries, as in a 'catalogue' of materials relating generally to the subject area, are not acceptable.

 **Activity**

In the articles and theses in your sample, what is the relative balance in the use of literature between the following?

• To carry arguments or counter-arguments forward.
• To identify a gap in knowledge or understanding.
• To demonstrate a knowledge of the field.

## Originality

All institutions require PhD theses to show originality, which can be in terms of the research design or of the outcomes of the research; it can have a single major aspect or several minor ones. Originality is the subject of Chapter 15, and here is not the place to be concerned with it to any extent. However, you may be reassured to know that the originality as well as the logic and coherence of the theses in your sample, as with all theses, almost certainly will have emerged out of hindsight. More is said on this in Chapter 18.

## Significance

All institutions require PhD theses to be significant contributions to the field. That some theses achieve this is beyond question. With others, however, it can be a matter of opinion and debate, guided by normal expectations in the field of study concerned.

## Objectivity and subjectivity

New research students often feel that a piece of research ought to be entirely objective. This is not at all so, and if your work is in any way concerned with, for example, small samples of people, then their subjectivity is a fundamental aspect of it. Addressing subjectivity starts with setting the research methodology within suitable 'research paradigms' (see Box 5.7).

---

**Box 5.7**   The meaning of 'paradigm'

*A paradigm is an overriding viewpoint that shapes ideas and actions ... A paradigm shift occurs when ideas and practices taken more or less for granted under the old paradigm are reassessed under the new. Such a shift occurred in the sixteenth century when Copernicus claimed that the Earth went round the Sun, and in the nineteenth century with Darwin's theory of natural selection.*

(McArthur, 1992)

Modifying this definition gives: A research paradigm is an overriding viewpoint that shapes ideas and actions about the conduct of research and the validity of its findings.

---

A research paradigm is a 'school of thought' or 'a way of thinking' about the nature of truth as it can be realized from a piece of research. Different writers use various names when discussing research paradigms even when they are broadly similar, and consequently it is impossible to say how many there are. This book will simplify them into two, which it will call the 'scientific' research paradigm and the 'interpretivist' research paradigm.*

* The term 'scientific' research paradigm has been in general use for a considerable time; the term 'interpretivist' research paradigm has been coined comparatively recently and is due to Denzin and Lincoln (1994, p. 536).

The scientific research paradigm can only be used where the variables that affect the work can be identified, isolated and measured – and often also manipulated – which is how research in the natural sciences normally operates. Researchers who can work in this paradigm are fortunate because their findings are generally objective and reproducible – which is why the scientific research paradigm is held in such high esteem. Data in the scientific research paradigm is always numerical, i.e. quantitative.

However, the scientific research paradigm is almost always inappropriate for research involving small numbers of people. Then variables, such as 'hungry', 'happy' or 'slept well', which cannot be measured in quantifiable terms, become extremely influential. To set such research in the scientific research paradigm, their effects would have to cancel one another out, which would be a fair assumption only with a very large sample of people. With a small sample, all the relevant variables do not cancel one another out; neither can they be readily identified or measured, let alone isolated and held constant while others are varied experimentally. Then research has to be set in the interpretivist research paradigm. This is more like establishing a verdict in a court of law than conducting an experiment in a laboratory. The evidence can be circumstantial and even where there are eye-witness accounts, doubt can always be cast on the veracity or reliability of the observers. A verdict must be reached on what is reasonable, i.e. the weight of evidence one way or the other and the power of the argument. The truth is not a mathematical certainty. Data gathered within the interpretivist research paradigm may be quantitative, as for example in coded questionnaires, but the emphasis is on exploration and insight rather than experiment.

The scientific research paradigm is appropriate for research touched by human behaviour where the data is quantitative – that is, capable of being measured – for example the number of children in certain named schools; where the sample is sufficiently large for the effects of individual variables effectively to cancel out; and where the data can be manipulated mathematically and statistically. Then the emphasis is on mathematical validity.

Research paradigms tend to be associated with particular disciplines, but even within some disciplines there can be intense rivalries between individuals who have loyalties to a particular research paradigm. This is because the research paradigm in which a piece of research is conducted affects the nature of the truth that it uncovers.

Alternative terms for research paradigms which are broadly similar to the scientific research paradigm are: quantitative, traditional, experimental, hard, reductionist, prescriptive, psychometric – and there are probably others. Alternative terms for research paradigms which are broadly similar to the interpretivist paradigm are: qualitative, soft, non-traditional, holistic, descriptive, anthropological, naturalistic, illuminative – and again there are probably others.

Different parts of a complex investigation may need to be set in different research paradigms. In the interpretivist research paradigm, there are various techniques for minimizing subjectivity, and, in due course, your supervisor will advise you on those which are most appropriate for your work. The Further Reading section references works on research paradigms.

### (■)  Activity

If the articles and theses in your sample are concerned in any way with the vagaries of human behaviour, check on the various ways in which they deal with possible subjectivity of results.

Do any of the articles fall into the trap of ignoring subjectivity by focusing on what can be measured and measuring it, even though the central aspects of the research problem ought in fact to be variables which cannot be measured?

### (■)  Discussion of activity

Because the scientific research paradigm is so highly esteemed, people often try to use it even where it is not appropriate. In this connection there is a well-known analogy which is reported in various forms, about a person looking for what he has lost under a lamp post, because that is where the light is, even though he knows that he lost it somewhere else. Working inappropriately within the scientific research paradigm is no less absurd, even though it is often done.                                                                (■)

# 6 INTERACTING WITH YOUR SUPERVISOR(S)

*When a supervisor accepts a student, whatever the formal rules may be, both have entered into an implied moral contract which lasts until one of the three – supervisor, student, or research undertaking – expires.*

(National Postgraduate Committee, 1995)

## The importance of the student–supervisor relationship

The relationship between a research student and a supervisor can be a precious thing. Supervisors and research students work closely together over a number of years. Mutual respect and trust can and should develop, together with a working relationship that can continue, as between equals, long after the completion of the research degree. It is in your own interests as a research student to develop and nurture this relationship. At the very least, only a highly unusual

---

**Box 6.1** How to recognize an outstanding supervisor

The following conclusion was reached in an Australian research project which looked at postgraduate work in a range of academic departments. It has a face validity which suggests universal applicability.

*One of the hallmarks of outstanding supervisors appeared . . . to be that their students felt driven very hard to impress them.*

(Parry and Hayden, 1994, p. 75)

student successfully completes a research degree if the relationship with a supervisor is poor.

There are two aspects to developing and nurturing the relationship with a supervisor, and they are valid irrespective of how many supervisors you may have. One is professional and starts with finding out the respective roles of research students and supervisors, as laid out formally by the institution. The other is interpersonal and involves treating a supervisor as a human being, who has strengths and weaknesses, personal satisfactions and disappointments, good days and bad days, just like everyone else.

In this chapter and in the rest of the book, the single term 'supervisor' is used for the individual staff member who has day-to-day responsibility for you. Where you have additional supervisory support, you will need to adapt what you read for your own circumstances.

## The roles and responsibilities of supervisors and research students

Essentially, a supervisor's principal professional responsibility is to help his or her research students to develop into individuals who think and behave as academic researchers in the field of study concerned. This involves advising them, encouraging them and warning them, according to the situation. Students' principal responsibilities are concerned with taking responsibility for their own work. Some ramifications and implications are considered shortly.

The extracts in Boxes 6.2 and 6.3 respectively lay out the responsibilities of supervisors and research students, as recommended by the National Postgraduate Committee. These guidelines are useful to stimulate discussion and thought, but they may not be right for all supervisor–student partnerships, and you and your supervisor may already have something better in operation.

---

**Box 6.2** The (recommended) responsibilities of the supervisor

These responsibilities are, according to National Postgraduate Committee (1995, p. 5), as follows:

1 *The supervisor should have knowledge of a student's subject area and/or theoretical approach to be applied.*
2 *If a student's work goes significantly outside the supervisor's field, the supervisor and the department should be responsible*

for putting the student in touch with specialists either inside or outside the institution who could help.

3 There should be regular supervisory sessions between students and supervisor, ideally at least once a fortnight. It is usually advisable to arrange for the time of the next meeting at the end of each session.

4 Supervisory sessions will naturally vary in length but on average they should last for at least one hour. It is important that they should be largely uninterrupted by telephone calls, personal callers or departmental business.

5 If the student has an urgent problem, the supervisor should deal with the matter over the telephone or arrange a meeting at short notice.

6 The supervisor should read and critically comment on written work as it is produced.

7 The supervisor should assist new students to plan their time, draw up a programme of work and monitor their subsequent progress. The supervisor should be aware of the requirements of some funding bodies and/or institutions that renewal of funding can depend on successful upgrade from MPhil to PhD and should help students on such contracts to plan their work accordingly.

8 The supervisor should submit a report to the Postgraduate Study Committee every six months and keep the student's record file maintained.

9 The supervisor must ensure that the student is made aware if either progress or the standard of work is unsatisfactory, and arrange any necessary supportive action.

10 It is the responsibility of the supervisor to ensure that the data, results and information garnered by the student during their research is freely available to the student.

11 Research students should be eligible to attend free of charge any course of lectures run in the institution. Supervisors should advise on courses which may complement their field of research.

12 The supervisor should take an active part in introducing the student to meetings of learned societies, seminars and workshops and to other research workers in the field. The supervisor should give advice on publication and put the student in touch with publishers where appropriate. The supervisor should give advice on writing up the research work in the form of papers and the final thesis. The supervisor should ensure that the student receives due recognition for their contribution to any publication, according to the usual conventions in the field.

*13 The supervisor must make clear the institution's regulations governing the nomination of the external and internal examiners for a student's viva (oral). Subject to the decision of the relevant bodies, the supervisor should arrange a mutually convenient date for the examiners and the student for the viva.*

**Box 6.3**  The (recommended) responsibilities of the research student

These responsibilities are, according to National Postgraduate Committee (1995, p. 6), as follows:

*1 By the end of the first year (the first 18 months in the case of part-time students) (subject to specific, published departmental practices which may, because of the nature of the subject, vary from this model) the student should have defined the area of research, become acquainted with the background knowledge required, completed the literature review and have a framework for the future progress of the research with a timetable for the next 2 or 3 years (3 or 4 years in the case of part-time students). The student should have produced a 'substantial' amount of written work, even if only in draft form. 'Substantial' should be defined by the supervisor or department at the outset.*
*2 The responsibility is on students to have their own topics that they would like to discuss with the supervisor.*
*3 Students must submit written work regularly to their supervisors.*
*4 Students should take note of the guidance and feedback from their supervisors.*
*5 Students should generally produce all material in word-processed or typed form. Material containing complex equations may be exempted, but the presentation of such must be neat and legible.*
*6 Students must inform their supervisor of other people with whom their work is being discussed.*
*7 It is the student's responsibility to seek out the supervisor. Any serious problems a student has with the supervisor, including those of access, should be initially taken up by the student with the supervisor at the time.*

## The developing nature of supervision

Many new research students tend to expect their supervisors to tell them what to do. Indeed, this may be justified where the work is tied into a group project and bounded by the efficient use of expensive and heavily used equipment. Where it is not, students may wait for their supervisors to tell them what to do because they think that demonstrating dependence in this way also demonstrates respect. Fortunately, good supervisors realize that they have to wean many research students gradually into independence, and they may provide a well-defined task as something on which they can both build – perhaps a pilot project of some sort. If this is what your supervisor does, it may give you a sense of security, but things are unlikely to carry on that way. Many people would argue that they ought not to carry on that way.

At the other extreme, some supervisors toss out a multitude of ideas at the first meeting, which can be overwhelming. If this happens to you, just realize that the ideas are merely possibilities for you to consider, not tasks that you necessarily have to do. Your best course of action is probably to make a note of them and take them away to think about, considering which ones are fundamental to research design in your field and which ones are alternative possibilities for ways forward. It is you and you alone who have to be intimately involved with your work over the next few years, and it is essential that you design it so that it appeals to you, as well as being acceptable to your supervisor.

As your work progresses, supervisions should become two-way dialogues. Your supervisor will expect you to develop your own ideas – which may have to be bounded by the needs of group research – but will want to discuss them with you, to give advice and to warn in good time against possible dangers. It is not a sound interpretation of 'independence' for research students to continue along their own way, on the mistaken assumption that they do not need supervisions.

Since research means going beyond published work and developing something new, your relationship with your supervisor must accommodate the natural and inevitable fact that you will eventually come to know more about your work than your supervisor. You will need to become comfortable with this and with engaging him or her in academic debate.

## Arranging meetings with a supervisor

Some departments distinguish between formal supervisions and informal meetings; and they have specific policies about timings and durations of the former, often laying them out in advance for an entire programme of study and requiring specific documents to be completed at each meeting. Other departments do not make the distinction, and often leave arrangements for the mode of operation of meetings unspecified. The former is more common in fields of study where long-term planning is feasible; and the latter is more common where the direction of each stage of the work emerges from the findings of an earlier stage.

Where meeting schedules are not laid out, many supervisors are torn in two directions as far as scheduling supervisions is concerned, and it is helpful for you to understand why. On the one hand supervisors want to do what they can to be supportive, but on the other they do not want to interfere on the grounds that independent research students ought to take the initiative when they need to discuss work which is, after all, their own. This latter view is reinforced by the formal dictate of most institutions that it is the responsibility of the student to take the initiative in raising problems or difficulties, however elementary they may seem, and to agree a schedule of meetings with the supervisor.

The practical way forward is for you to take steps early on to find out how scheduling supervisions is likely to work best for the unique partnership between your supervisor and yourself. It is polite to wait a while, to see if there are departmental codes of practice and to give your supervisor time to make suggestions, but if this does not happen, raise the matter yourself. The following activity provides a checklist of the crucial issues.

(■)    **Activity**

---

Find out how comfortable you and your supervisor are with the following ways of arranging meetings:

• Dates and times of meetings are arranged a considerable time ahead according to departmental requirements.

   – Are there distinctions there between formal and informal meetings?

• You take the initiative by sending in a request for a meeting.

– Does it help your supervisor if you provide something in writing about what you want to talk about so that it can be considered before you meet?

– Or does your supervisor prefer to cut down the burden of inessential reading and react to you on the spot when you meet?

• Your supervisor timetables regular meetings irrespective of whether there is anything new or special to discuss.

• If either you or your supervisor think there is any reason to meet, one of you arranges it when you next happen to see each other.

• You simply turn up at your supervisor's office in the expectation of him or her having time for you.

• Some other arrangement. What?

How are you expected to go about setting up an additional meeting in an emergency?

---

(■)  **Discussion of activity**

Each of the above possibilities will suit some partnerships of research students and supervisors, but some will be intensely disagreeable to some supervisors. So you and your supervisor must develop a mode of working that suits you both.

Supervisors are busy people, and their load of work is increasing all the time. So be sensitive about taking up your supervisor's time. Remember, though, that legally the responsibility for not taking matters up with your supervisor is likely to be yours, and that if you neglect to communicate ideas and findings to your supervisor, you may overlook obvious interpretations and wander into dead-ends. Supervisors who feel that they are being worried unnecessarily should say so.

Frequency of meetings also has to be considered, where there are no departmental requirements. Some supervisors like to see full-time students three times a term and part-time students twice a term; some much more often. Some supervisors like to have two or more meetings booked ahead in diaries, on the proviso that they can be cancelled nearer the time if there is no need to meet. Other supervisors feel that meetings should be set up flexibly, according to the needs of the student for supervision, which are likely to be greatest when the direction of the work is being decided and during the final stages of the writing-up.                                         (■)

## Taking notes during meetings with a supervisor

Research students need to have a record of what takes place during meetings with supervisors. This is for their own records (a topic considered further in Chapter 7), so that they can think the discussion over before taking action. Memory may not be enough. The record ought not merely to reflect topics discussed, advice given and decisions made, but also the degree of conviction behind them. Often ideas are presented on the off-chance rather than in the certainty that they might prove useful, and conclusions can have varying degrees of tentativeness.

Taking notes is a personal matter, and what suits one research student may not suit another. Students often find it gives them confidence to ask their supervisors if they may audio-tape supervisions, even if, in the event, they never find it necessary to listen to the tape. Not only does the tape give a verbatim record of ideas and conclusions, and the strength of feeling behind them, it also records forms of expression and explanation which may be superior to anything used so far, and which may be ideal for putting into reports and the thesis.

## Asking a supervisor for feedback and advice

Most research students are entirely satisfied with how their supervisor responds to their requests for feedback and advice; and any initial problems tend to sort themselves out as the relationship develops. You can help by understanding some of the pressures that your supervisor may be under, and acting accordingly.

Supervisors are human beings who are exceptionally busy and who may also be shy or inexperienced. Any of these may be reasons for unhelpful, throwaway remarks rather than considered responses. There are other possible reasons. For example, a supervisor may not want to stunt the development of your independence by rejecting your ideas. Or he or she may feel embarrassed at rejecting your ideas, perhaps because you are a mature student with an impressive career record, or because you are a colleague in the department. If you think that any of these may be the case, a good technique is not to ask for a reaction to a single idea. Suggest several alternatives. Then there is something to discuss and an implicit ground-rule is that some ideas will have to be rejected.

Overwork could be affecting a supervisor. If you think that this may be so, be sensitive about how you raise issues for discussion. He or she may react most favourably to a written outline of your ideas, to study and respond to at leisure or convenience. On the other hand, an informal chat, to ease interaction with burgeoning paperwork, may be more acceptable. In your own interests, you should find out.

It is a well-researched and accepted fact that people tend to reject ideas if they feel forced into quick decisions. If you think that this may be a problem when you interact with a supervisor, give him or her plenty of thinking time by outlining the situation and then suggesting that he or she might like to mull it over in readiness for talking again in a few days.

If you think that a supervisor may be suffering from the shyness of inexperience, put him or her at ease by asking for answers to simple questions, to which you may even already know the answers. If, of course, the problem is also overwork, this tactic would make matters worse rather than better.

## Responding to feedback and criticism from a supervisor

It is in your own interests that your supervisor gives full and comprehensive feedback on your work. This is difficult on both sides where the feedback is critical, and you need to help in every way you can.

Start by accepting that certain emotions are normal. You may be embarrassed at what you think your supervisor is seeing as your inadequacy, and you may be angry at how he or she appears to be misunderstanding you. Understandable as these emotions are, it is counter-productive to let them show, and the chances are that, when you calm down, you will realize that they were unjustified anyway.

So if it is necessary, mask negative emotions. Try to show gratitude that your supervisor is going to so much trouble to give the feedback, and to show interest in its content.

It is not necessary to agree with all the criticisms, either while they are being made or later. Only you know the ramifications for your own work and situation. So only when you have taken time to consider can you decide how much to accept, reject or adapt. Agreeing instantly with criticism indicates compliance and lack of independent thinking. Seek clarification if necessary and then say that you will go away and do some thinking, ready for talking again about any points that may need further discussion.

Only in exceptional circumstances is it sensible to launch into a justification of why the criticism is inappropriate. You may want to justify some points, but do this only when your supervisor has finished his or her say on that point. Then ask if he or she would like you to explain the reasons for what you did.

At the close of the meeting, reiterate your thanks. Say nothing more, other than general pleasantries.

## Handling unprofessional behaviour from a supervisor

Unprofessional behaviour from supervisors is rare. Nevertheless when it does happen, it can cause a great deal of distress to the research student who has to cope with it, particularly because of the implicit power relationship that accompanies it.

The behaviour may be due to some sort of prejudice – perhaps racism, sexism, ageism or some other '-ism'. Although institutions normally have – or state that they are working towards – equal opportunities policies, these are normally only of help when matters have already got out of hand. The best course of action for a research student is to realize that prejudice in highly intelligent and educated people is due to ignorance and/or a sense of inferiority. The way forward is to train them out of it by ignoring the insinuations and innuendoes, referring only to work and acting in words, dress and manner, totally professionally. Supervisors are unlikely to persist with attitudes and behaviour where research students supply ongoing evidence that these are inappropriate. Sadly, this course of action will take time. Support and advice should be available from other research students; the member of staff, if he or she exists, who has departmental responsibility for research students; the head of department; formal institutional documents and the students' union.

---

**Box 6.4**  A view, a comment and a counter-view on sexual harassment and relationships between academics and students

*[There are] principled reasons for avoiding staff-student love affairs, because of the power advantage lecturers have as assessors, as well as pragmatic reasons. 'You have to take into account the views of the student's peer group. Even if you think you are being as even-handed as possible I can guarantee you the peer group suspects there is favour.'*

(Mary Davis, as reported in *Times Higher Education Supplement*, 1995, p. 4)

*In the event of involvement in a relationship with a student, particularly when it is a romantic or sexual one, the member of staff is encouraged to declare it to an appropriate supervisor or colleague or to a third party designated by the university for the purpose after consultation with AUT.*

(From the code of conduct governing staff–student relationships, produced by the Women's Committee of the Association of University Teachers (AUT), as reported in Bristow, 1995)

*The [AUT] code has been adopted by a number of universities and while most students are unaware that it even exists, those students and lecturers on the receiving end are more than a little sceptical ... This view that female students are all really vulnerable little girls in need of attention is simply patronising.*

(Bristow, 1995)

---

Box 6.4 considers other forms of unprofessional behaviour, as does Box 11.1 in Chapter 11.

It is crucial to do whatever one can informally early on, rather than formally later once things may have got out of hand. Appeals in connection with equal opportunities policies are difficult to substantiate and stressful; and rightly or wrongly, the wronged person may be regarded as a troublemaker.

## Changing a supervisor

Although most student–supervisor partnerships work well, there are those which do not. Perhaps there is continuing unprofessional behaviour as discussed in the previous section; or a clash of personalities; or a lack of interest. Perhaps a supervisor does not seem to have adequate expertise in the subject area; perhaps he or she does not seem to respect arguments and judgement when the research student, after genuine and lengthy consideration, feels that they are valid. If giving it time does not work, diplomacy is needed. Not only is it impolite to compromise a supervisor; it is probably pointless and is likely, however justified, to discredit the person doing it in the eyes of others.

If a change of supervisor does seem inevitable, find out as diplomatically as possible what the procedures are. Sources of advice are the member of staff, if he or she exists, who has departmental responsibility for research students, the head of department, formal institutional documents and the students' union. The final recourse would be to make enquiries at the Registry.

Again, it is crucial to do whatever one can informally early on, rather than formally later once things may have got out of hand. Some institutions do allow appeals on the grounds of inadequate supervision, but most do not. Whatever the validity of appeals, they are stressful, time-consuming and usually public; and sadly in the eyes of the world, 'mud sticks', even to innocent parties. At best, research students will recover no more than lost fees.

## Getting a co-supervisor

Research students whose work is collaborative or cross-disciplinary may have had more than one supervisor from the outset. Other research students may identify a need for an additional supervisor only as the work develops and steps outside the expertise of their current supervisor. Being supervised by more than one supervisor may work well in some circumstances, but reports of it working badly are so widespread that co-supervision needs to be considered very carefully before being adopted.

The misgivings do not apply where the co-supervisor is merely overseeing the normal supervisor–student interactions because the day-to-day supervisor is inexperienced. Neither do they apply to backup supervisors – individuals who agree to help while the day-to-day supervisor is away or ill – so that work is not delayed. Neither do they apply to team, panel or committee supervision, where the roles of the individual members are negotiated and formally agreed at the outset.

The misgivings apply where a co-supervisor is brought in because the work has developed or is likely to develop outside the expertise of the original supervisor, but where the individual roles and re-sponsibilities of each supervisor are not fully discussed, agreed and defined at the outset. Neither co-supervisor fully understands the expertise of the other – which is why there are two of them – and this puts tremendous burdens on the research student who has to integrate the understanding of both and satisfy both. The research student all too often ends up satisfying neither, and each co-super-visor can tacitly abdicate responsibility to the other. A single super-visor, on the other hand, carries full professional and personal – although not legal – responsibility for the research student. With such support, the research student is in a good position to complete the programme of work satisfactorily. So it is worth thinking care-fully before agreeing to joint supervision in a situation where the roles of the co-supervisors are not formalized. One alternative, when your work seems to be moving outside the expertise of your super-visor, is that you both visit experts and learn together about the new area. Another alternative is that you direct your research to stay within the expertise of your supervisor.

## The formal position

The respective duties and responsibilities of supervisors, research students and the institution are normally laid out formally in insti-tutional documents, the contents of which, for most institutions, may come as a surprise to research students. In particular, the for-mal and legal responsibilities are unlikely to lie where you may expect. So it is very important to have sight of the documents and to read them thoroughly. Use the following activity as a checklist. Without it you may find out too late that you have been labouring under the illusion of misassigned responsibilities.

### ▣  Activity

Study your institution's documentation on the duties and respons-ibilities of supervisors, research students and the institution. In par-ticular, note the formal position regarding:

- who takes responsibility for the thesis being ready to be examined;

- rights of appeal against inadequate supervision.

---

(■)  **Discussion of activity**

In most institutions, it is the student's responsibility to decide when the thesis is ready to be examined, even though of course the supervisor will give an opinion. There is thus no recourse, other than the formal appeals procedures already mentioned, if the degree is not awarded. So, if you see things going wrong, it is in your own interests to act in good time to do something about them yourself. (■)

# 7  KEEPING RECORDS

*Meet it is I set it down.*

(Shakespeare, *Hamlet*, act I, scene v)

## The importance of keeping records

Supervisors, departments and funding bodies normally keep full records on their students, for their own use and for reasons connected with quality assurance. They may also provide students with pro formas for keeping their own records. As these are likely to be concerned primarily with events such as formal meetings with supervisors, progress reports and presentation of seminars, it is important for research students to keep their own full, detailed and personalized records. This is true irrespective of field of study.

How to keep your records is a matter of personal preference, guided by the norms of your field of study, the experience of other workers in similar fields and the requirements of your department. You will not regret investing time and effort in looking for and setting up systems that seem right for you. This chapter considers some options.

## Purposes of keeping records

Your choice of system for keeping your records must depend on the purposes to which you may need to put them. Some purposes are common for all research students irrespective of field of study; others will depend on the field of study and on plans for future career and professional development. Here are some possible purposes of keeping records; the list is not intended to be exhaustive.

- To preserve data that you collect, for later processing.
- To preserve information that you read, for later processing.
- To preserve information about what you do and how long you spend doing it, as an aid to reflection; to keep on track and to suggest ways of improving your time management.
- To provide information for progress reports and the thesis.
- To provide ideas for future directions of the work.
- To provide information for setting targets, possibly including provisional dates and planning schedules.
- To document demarcations between your work and the work of others in group projects. (You will need to be able to show this unambiguously in your thesis.)
- To deliver that information back to you, as and when you wish to retrieve it.
- To satisfy supervisors or departments, where they require such records.
- To show records or examples of achievement to potential employers.
- To submit, where applicable, with an application for chartered status with a professional body.

(■)    **Activity**

Which of the above purposes and what additional purposes might you have for keeping records of your ongoing work?

## Ways of keeping records

Before deciding on a way or ways of recording your work, carefully consider the purposes to which you wish to put the records. Also bear in mind the inevitable compromise between ease of putting in the information and ease of retrieving it. For example, a particularly straightforward way of inputting information would be to keep hand-written notes on scraps of paper. Yet this would be the least straightforward for quick and easy retrieval, as it would require sorting through to find what is there and interpreting handwriting. The choice is personal: to go for ease of inputting, ease of retrieval or a balance somewhere between them.

Of the variety of possible ways of keeping records of work, the most obvious is log books or diaries. In some fields of study, it is usual for these to be in a pre-bound form so that every mistake and doodle is recorded in sequence alongside the more formalized records. The idea is that such apparently extraneous material meant something when originally done, and even though its significance may not be obvious at the time, it can turn out to be important later. In other fields of study, it may be considered appropriate to keep a more formalized diary, either using one of the day-to-a-page sorts available from stationers or as many looseleaf pages for a day as required, filed in sequence. Log books and diaries should include such things as:

- what you do, and where, how and why you do it, with dates, possibly with an indication of time spent;
- what you read (see later in this chapter);
- what data you collect, how you process it and what the outcomes are;
- special achievements, dead-ends and surprises;
- what you think or feel about what is happening;
- any thoughts that come into your mind that may be relevant for your research;
- what your supervisor's reactions are, possibly in note form or as appended audio-cassette tapes;
- anything else that is influencing you.

One possibility for recording data is to use a computerized data base. Although it may require time and effort to set up and slightly more discipline when inputting, retrieval is straightforward and rapid, irrespective of the amount of data. Where such records include data on individuals, they are subject to the Data Protection Act. Each institution should have someone who is responsible for ensuring that the provisions of that Act are observed and who may be consulted for advice in this connection.

Another possibility is to draft parts of the thesis as you go along, within a draft outline. Although it is not possible to envisage in advance the exact form of a thesis, it may be possible, where the objectives and plan of the research are unlikely to change, for a general outline to be prepared, once preliminary work has been completed. This can serve as a map to guide you. Although at the outset it will contain only a few major landmarks and will change considerably as the work progresses, it may still be recognizable in the final thesis. The thesis outline can provide a basic shape to your work; it facilitates thinking about what you are doing: why you are doing it, what you ought to do next and what the outcomes are likely to be. All are powerful motivators.

If you keep your records in any form on a computer, it is essential to keep backups on your own floppy disks. Most experienced researchers can tell horrific stories of how days or even months of work were lost when a computer crashed and they had not bothered to keep backups. Box 7.1 tells a typical story.

Before deciding on the best method or methods of record-keeping for you, talk to several people, your supervisor and other research students, who keep records of their work in different ways. Use the following activity as a checklist.

---

**Box 7.1**   Keep back-up copies! Sheila's story

*From the start I was aware that I should keep a copy of my work on back-up disk in case of accidents. However, perhaps as with plague, famine, war and terminal illnesses, we like to imagine that they happen to other people but never to ourselves. It was only after I lost a whole week's work, which simply disappeared from a disk, that I now make not only one but three back-up disks of each chapter.*

(Salmon, 1992, p. 112)

---

● **Activity**

---

How do other workers in the field keep records of their work?

How well do they think that different methods help them to:

• retrieve data later?

• reflect on their time and resource management?

• get ideas for future work?

• set targets for future work?

What advantages and disadvantages do they see in how they keep their records, and what general advice do they give?

---

(■)    **Discussion of activity**

The detail and frequency of updating of your records must depend on your personal preferences, guided by what has proved useful to other workers in the field.                                            (●)

## Recording achievements in a portfolio

It is a good idea to keep a special box or drawer of information from which you can select items to demonstrate your achievements to different interest groups: perhaps a departmental meeting; a meeting of a professional body; or an interview for future employment. The collection is generally referred to as a 'portfolio', although confusingly the term also tends to be used for each different set of items that you select to put into your bag (portfolio) for each type of use.

Keeping a portfolio really is an excellent idea. Employers and accreditation bodies are placing increasing emphasis on them, and quite generally people are far more likely to be impressed by seeing what you have done than by just hearing or reading about it. So get used to collecting items that may be useful. Here are some possibilities to stimulate your thinking, but they are not exhaustive.

• Your current curriculum vitae.
• Any letters or documents that may serve as testimonials to your

work. It is often worth requesting these in writing whenever some-
one praises or thanks you in connection with work.
- Copies of progress reports.
- Statements of courses or other training undertaken.
- Fliers or programmes for meetings, seminars or conferences attended.
- Notes of participation in professional body activities.
- Notes of participation in team/community activities.
- Fliers or programmes for any teaching or laboratory demonstration undertaken.
- Any agreed study plans with records of amendments made to it.
- Diaries or formal notes of meetings with supervisor(s).
- Departmental or subject-based codes of practice, where relevant, with which you comply.
- Any permits, licences or agreements which you have been awarded.

(■)  **Activity**

What have you got tucked away that could usefully form part of
your portfolio?

What are you likely to do in the near future that could contribute
to your portfolio?

## Keeping records from the literature

Your choice of system for keeping records of what you read must
again depend on the purposes to which you may need to put the
records. Here are some possibilities:

- To provide a record of the background knowledge relating to your topic.
- To provide a record of the theories and methods of analysis generally used for enquiring into your field of study.
- To provide a record of the primary sources in the field, as recognized by previous researchers.
- To deliver information back to you, as and when you want to retrieve it.
- To support various streams of argument and counter-argument in your thesis.

There are various ways of keeping records from the literature. Data-base computer packages can be useful. Once set up for bibliographic entry and retrieval, they throw up a checklist of all the information that is needed for a full reference of any item, and they allow quick and easy retrieval by author, date, keywords, etc.

Some supervisors still recommend index cards, suitably cross-referenced, which is effectively the manual equivalent of a data-base manager system. The space required for storage can be a problem, as can the reordering into new categories, the need for which will become very likely as work progresses.

Alternatively a word processor can be used, with the information typed or scanned in. Information can be entered in chronological or any other order, and retrieval is with the 'find' command on any words which may seem useful at the time or at any later date.

Copyright law generally permits photocopying of individual articles for personal use for study and scholarship, but it is a prime example of easy inputting into your records not being the same as easy retrieval. At some stage the photocopies need to be read and processed.

There is no completely satisfactory way of keeping records from the literature because it is seldom possible to know at the time precisely how the item or quotation might best be used, if indeed it can be used at all. Hence difficult decisions have to be made about how much to record and with what keywords. There is no formalized procedure which can entirely support the burden of this, and there is no substitute for a mind that can provide a partial retrieval system of its own. The sheer size of the literature makes it impossible to keep personal records of everything, so it may be best to start with an overview of what sorts of thing that can be found where.

Before deciding what is best for you, talk to your supervisor, other research students and possibly other academic staff, who keep their literature records in different ways. Use the following activity as a stimulus.

**Activity**

How do other workers in the field keep records of their literature searches?

What advantages and disadvantages do they find with their method?

How do other workers deal with the difficulty of the sheer size of the literature?

 **Discussion of activity**

However you eventually decide to keep records from the literature, they should give complete references, as indicated in Chapter 5, so that items can be found again if necessary and so that they can be properly cited in the thesis.

# 8 PLANNING AHEAD

*If your supervisor does not believe in planning, then plan to change your supervisor.*

(James Irvine, personal communication, 1994)

## The importance of planning

Irrespective of your field of study, as a research student you need to map out some sort of plan for your programme of work ahead. Such a plan can prevent you from spending too long on certain activities because you enjoy them, or not attending to others which are unappealing; can provide a sense of security in that where you are now and where you are going, have been thought about and are documented; is something to display to a supervisor and others as a basis for discussion; can ease any anxiety by externalizing concerns rather than having to keep carrying them and manipulating them in your mind; and should provide a basis for reflection so that, having seen where your previous plans may have been unrealistic, you can plan more effectively next time round.

Detailed plans inevitably need regular amendment (see Box 8.1). How much and how often tend to depend on the nature of the work. They can normally be made on longer time-scales where

---

**Box 8.1**   Planning does not mean blueprinting

*Here, then, is perhaps the first lesson of research; it can, in a very general way, be planned, but not blueprinted. One simply does not know what one is going to discover. These discoveries may lead to a complete change of direction.*

(Berry, 1986, p. 5)

---

**Box 8.2**   Planning a programme of work

*A Programme of Work is essential. The research topic should be agreed as soon as possible and a programme drawn up and approved by the supervisor during the first [term or] semester. The supervisor should ensure that the student is aware of the basis of the supervisor's assessment of progress and understands the amount of work involved. The programme must include:*

- *a provisional outline of the thesis, which should be expanded as the course progresses*
- *a statement of the research and sources to be examined*
- *a provisional timetable for carrying out the research and writing the thesis.*

*There will be some alterations as research proceeds and hypotheses change but every effort should be made to ensure that the programme's basic outline remains intact. Where revisions are made, a clear record of the need for revisions and the effect on the timescale should be retained by the student in the department's student file.*

(National Postgraduate Committee, 1995, p. 9)

---

objectives can be clearly laid out in advance, and where a team is working on a single large project. They can normally be made only on fairly short time-scales where the direction of any one stage of the work is based on recognizing and grasping opportunities which present themselves as the work progresses and which cannot be foreseen; where understanding grows holistically; or where changes of direction are frequent, normal or imposed through circumstances.

This chapter is about planning your programme of work (see Box 8.2). It is not about developing a research methodology. That has to rely on knowing and understanding the use of the various research strategies, methods and techniques that are normal in your field – and possibly outside it – and matching them to the needs of your particular topic or research problem. For this, only your supervisor and others in your field can help.

## Departmental planning schedules

The norms of research in some disciplines are such that some departments can and do provide their research students with a common framework of essential or required actions, with projected dates for the full three-year period of full-time research. These may be primarily events, such as formal meetings with supervisors, progress reports and presentation of seminars. Or they may extend to lengthier activities, such as studying the literature, negotiating the research plan, collecting data, writing reports, etc., each with a projected time-span. Such a framework can form a useful basis for planning. However, many disciplines require more flexibility because the type and direction of work required at any stage depend on the outcome of a previous stage. Then the planning has to be on shorter time-scales and more ongoing.

(■) **Activity**

Does your department suggest a common plan for the work of its research students? If so:

• Over what timescale does this operate?

• How detailed is it?

• How much do supervisors expect research students to veer away from it?

• What do you think about its usefulness?

(■)  **Discussion of activity**

Although plans are both helpful and essential for all research students irrespective of the nature of their work, the detail and duration of validity of the plans have to be in accordance with the type
of research, and are likely to differ considerably from one discipline
to another. This is exemplified in the document on postgraduate
research from the former Science and Engineering Research Council,
which offered a rough general plan for moving through a PhD. A
parallel document, originating at about the same time, from the
Economic and Social Science Research Council offered no such general plan.                                                         (■)

## The project management approach to planning

Project management is a formalized approach to planning which
can be as simple or as sophisticated as users care to make it.

A basic technique, which would repay the time and effort of any
research student in any field of study, would be a bar chart of activities marked on a time-scale, as shown in Figure 8.1. This illustrates
the use of colour (or shade) coding and shaped symbols. Different
shadings indicate:

- tasks expected to occupy all of the allocated time – in Figure 8.1,
  scanning the journals and writing the report;
- short tasks to be done at some stage during the allocated time –
  in Figure 8.1, meeting the visiting professor;
- tasks which must fit the allocated slot of time if they are to be
  done at all because they link in with arrangements which are
  firmly fixed – in Figure 8.1, attending the conference.

Different symbols indicate when something has to be completed.
The symbols are known as milestones and the 'something' as a
'deliverable'. In Figure 8.1, the deliverable is the report and the
milestone is the date it is to be handed in.

Figure 8.1 is a simple bar chart which any research student, working alone, could sketch out for him- or herself. Much more sophisticated project management packages can be run by computer, and
can manage the interacting work of individuals in a team and the
anticipated use of resources. You will probably only want to move
to one of these if your supervisor already operates one and is concerned that everyone involved should be able to see the progress of
everyone else at a glance, together with the usage of resources.

Bar charts are snapshots which capture how things are, or are

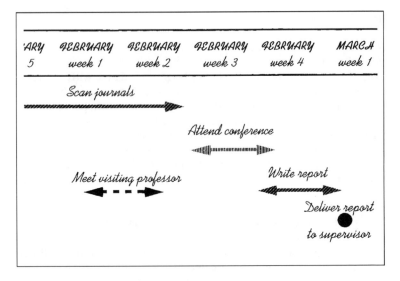

*Figure 8.1*

expected to be, at a moment in time. They will rapidly become out of date and need revision, because the unanticipated is in the very nature of research. They are none the less useful for all the reasons given in at the beginning of this chapter.

There is another technique which may be useful for students who feel that they do not know where to start among a sea of activities, or cannot manage to sequence their work effectively. This can be a common problem which results in certain aspects of work having to be held up because they rely on the results of other work which are not yet ready. Some students, with some types of research, can manage these problems in their heads, or find that they clarify themselves during the process of simple planning. However, project management offers a technique which can be useful, known as 'critical path analysis'. It enables tasks to be arranged into a sequence such that none will be held up because those on which they rely are not yet complete. The technique involves noting each task on a sheet of paper and then drawing arrows between them, linking them together in the order in which one relies on another. This may involve a certain amount of trial and error and possibly also, if one cares about aesthetic appearance, redrawing with tasks positioned differently on the page. Where there is considerable interrelationship between tasks, critical path diagrams will be more like networks than linear paths.

⬛  **Activity**

Make a bar chart for the next stage of your work in the style of Figure 8.1. Include:

- Key tasks and periods over which they have to be done.
- Milestones and deliverables – your own or any that may be imposed.

Annotate the bar chart with:

- The resources you want or need to use at each stage, together with their availability and cost.
- When and how your work links with and depends on input from other people.

How far ahead did you feel it reasonable to plan and how realistic or helpful did you find the planning?

If you feel uncertain about where to start any stage of your work, see if developing a critical path network might help.

**Discussion of activity**

It is likely that some sort of project management approach will be useful to some extent in your work. How useful will depend on the nature of your work.    ■

## Developing a style of plan for your own use

The ways in which most people develop and document their plans of work are highly personal, guided by the ideas and standard approaches of others in similar fields, and refined through their own experience.

■ **Activity**

---

Discuss planning techniques with other research students and your supervisor(s) and develop a style that suits you.

Practise and refine this through use.

---

■ **Discussion of activity**

Developing a method of planning is an ongoing activity and you may never feel that you have it quite right for your sort of work. This hardly matters because the act of progressively refining plans should markedly improve your work and your attitude towards it.    ■

## Identifying what is to go into your plan

If you are working alone in an area where others are not closely involved, your problem may be to identify the activities that need to go into your plan. Any of the creative thinking techniques of Chapter 16 can help.

(■)  **Activity**

Look at Chapter 16 and note the various techniques for creative thinking. Try some of them to develop ideas for the activities that ought to go into your plan. With the mind map technique, suitable spokes might be 'required outcomes', 'deadlines', 'resources', 'other people', but there are many possibilities.

## Planning extended work away from the institution

Planning for extended work away from home base requires special attention because, if not done properly, lack of finance and lack of opportunity may mean that there can be no second chance to have another go. Then the only way to recover is to take on a new research direction, with all the associated losses of time.

The following activity lists some of the planning issues to consider. Use it as a checklist for what is relevant for your planning if you have to work away from the institution for an extended period.

(■)  **Activity**

If your anticipated work is at some considerable distance from the institution, particularly if it is overseas, what plans do you intend to make, or have you made, for the following?

• Financing your travel, accommodation and living expenses while away. How far in advance ought you to start organizing this?

• Arranging meetings with individuals or access to buildings or resources at the new location. How far in advance ought you to start organizing this? Who needs to be contacted?

- Identifying someone to talk things over with while you are away. When should you contact them to get their agreement?

- Keeping in touch with your supervisor.

- Backup data collection if the intended source of data becomes unavailable.

- Resources to take with you, such as money, stationery and equipment.

- Anything else.

Have you checked that the time you wish to spend away from the institution is allowed within institutional regulations?

(■)    **Discussion of activity**

No doubt supervisors will advise on planning for working over an
extended period away from the institution. However, if any of the
above points give cause for concern, do mention them specifically
to your supervisor. You may need to make alternative or backup
plans. It is usually too late to do so once on location.

It will be helpful to identify someone local who can act as a
mentor while you are away. Some knowledge of the subject is desirable, but it is not as important as sound, logical and creative thinking ability; a commitment to being supportive; and time to be so.
Provided that you can find such a person, your own creative thinking and academic training should help you cope with the unexpected, at least until you can get in touch with your supervisor.

Fax or e-mail is probably the quickest and cheapest way of keeping in touch with your supervisor. Or you can fax or phone a secretary to set up a time for a lengthy phone call.

Institutional regulations will state the proportion of time that has
to be spent 'on campus' for research degrees. Application for study
leave must normally be formally supported by the supervisor and
made to the Registry, and approval must be given before departure.

There will, of course, be other administrative issues relating to your
particular subject area and to the location of the work, and there
will certainly be methodological issues. These need to be considered
by you and your supervisor together.    (■)


## Coping with things not going according to plan

All research students seem to report that they had unusually bad
luck somewhere along the way that played havoc with their plans.
In fact it was probably not bad luck, or at least not in the way that
bad luck is usually understood. Instead it was and is a normal feature of research: perhaps equipment is not delivered on time or
breaks down; perhaps people are not available when wanted; perhaps crucial information centres are closed for refurbishment; perhaps an essential book takes weeks to filter through the inter-library
loan system. Then there is always illness. The list could be endless.

The way of coping with unpredictable delays is in two parts. Firstly,
build in 40% more time than you expect for everything, without
getting lulled into the sense of security that this allows a more laid-
back approach. Secondly, have a list to hand of all the other related
tasks that you always meant to do but never had time for or that
you mean to do at some stage in the future. Examples might be

visiting a library some distance away that specializes in something that might be relevant; producing neat diagrams or tables for reports or the thesis; writing a draft of a chapter of a thesis; going to see someone; or even a treat of some sort in the way of leisure activities or a short holiday. Then, when an unforeseen delay supplies time on your hands, use it for one of the items on the list.

(■)    **Activity**

---

Make three lists.

• Things to do with work that you always meant to get round to, but never quite managed

• Non-urgent things that it would be useful to do sometime in the future

• Treats

For each entry in each list, jot down a reasonable estimate of the time that would have to be available for it.

---

# 9 MANAGING YOURSELF AND YOUR TIME

*Dost thou love life, then do not squander time, for that's the stuff life is made of.*

(Benjamin Franklin, quoted in Tripp's *The International Thesaurus of Quotations*, 1976, p. 640, item 19)

## The importance of managing yourself and your time

It has been said that a research degree is 1% inspiration and 99% perspiration. The 1% inspiration relies on creativity and will be considered in Chapter 16. The 99% perspiration is the routine work, for example attending meetings, reading around the subject, gathering data, keeping records, writing drafts and then rewriting in the light of feedback. Although opinions differ about the relative magnitudes of the inspiration and the perspiration, the adage does stress that both are important and that the routine work is always likely to be much the greater in terms of outlay of time. This chapter considers some ideas which may be new to you for making routine work more efficient.

## Finding out where your time goes

It is a common experience that time seems to disappear and one wonders where it has gone and what has been achieved. Whereas this probably does no harm when it happens occasionally, something must be done about it if it becomes a regular occurrence. The answer lies in finding out where the time goes, to provide a basis for re-evaluating activities. Some people like to do this by keeping a diary over a period of time, logging the various activities in each day. The task can be an amusing and even essential activity, but it does take considerable time which the benefit may not repay. Nevertheless, you may like to try it for a short period or for certain days.

⬛  **Activity**

If you feel that time is disappearing without any noticeable achievements, keep some form of log of what you do. This can be as accurate or rough as you please or think you need.

Does the log show up any surprisingly large usages of time?

Do you think you need to make any major changes in your use of time?

⬛  **Discussion of activity**

There are no hard and fast rules on how to spend time as a research student. What matters is that you should be content with your own use of time. Do realize that time spent on leisure activities or talking to people is not necessarily time wasted. You need them to maintain your physical and mental health (see later in this chapter), and they can, as Chapters 11 and 16 explain, also help your work.

Box 9.1 shows how one chemistry student's time was spent.

**Box 9.1**  Use of time by one postgraduate research student in a chemistry department

This is a record of the use of work time in each year of the three-year studentship in chemistry of one particular research student. No implication is intended that it is a good or bad use of time or that the categories would be appropriate for everyone, or that it is necessarily worth the effort to keep such a detailed record. The interest lies in the claim that the record is genuine. No doubt use of time by other research students would be very different, even in a similar field of study. In other fields of study, it would almost certainly be markedly different.

| Activity | Note | First Year | Second Year | Third Year |
|---|---|---|---|---|
| | | *Hours* | | |
| Laboratory | a | 1600 | 1875 | 1705 |
| Lectures | b | 140 | 50 | 50 |
| Library | | 100 | 50 | 100 |
| Meetings | c | 95 | 95 | 50 |
| Reporting | d | 135 | 90 | 270 |
| Vacation | | 90 | 90 | 45 |
| Other | e | 50 | | 30 |

*The working year comprises 50 weeks of 5 days; each day of 9 hours. The total number of working hours is thus 2250 per year.*

*All information is rounded up to the nearest 5 hours.*

a  *Laboratory work involves work at the University and elsewhere (i.e. at the laboratory of the industrial sponsor).*

b  *Lectures include coursework (and the examination thereof) and research seminars.*

c  *Meetings include research group meetings and attendance at conferences.*

d  *Reporting includes writing quarterly reports and annual reports, the preparation of four oral presentations to research group meetings and a final lecture, and the preparation of the PhD thesis.*

e  *Other relates to absence through illness and other justifiable causes.*

*Presumably there is some virement here. Most research students work sometimes during some weekends.*

(Supplied by a supervisor in chemistry, who wishes to remain anonymous)

## Using time efficiently when supervisions and seminars are cancelled

Supervisions and seminars do sometimes have to be cancelled at short notice, and it is worth taking all possible steps to ensure that you are informed in good time, so that you use the time to best advantage.

 **Activity**

Whose responsibility is it to let you know if a supervision or seminar has to be cancelled at short notice?

Make sure that this person has your current contact telephone number.

## Matching the task to the time slot

Sometimes the urgency of certain tasks must dictate the order in which they have to be done. Although this may occasionally be unavoidable, it is seldom ideal. Firstly, it may mean that an important task has to be rushed; and secondly, it may be an inefficient use of a time slot. Try the following activity to get a feel for the benefits of bothering to match tasks to available time slots.

 **Activity**

Imagine that you have the following tasks ahead of you. If you like, replace them with tasks which fit better into your own type of research.

- Sticking stamps on to 100 envelopes.
- Making two five-minute personal telephone calls.
- Writing up notes of an interview you have conducted and analysing its meaning.

- Arranging a meeting to help another research student.
- 
- 

Arrange these tasks into your personal timetable for the next week or month, ensuring that the use of time is as efficient as possible.

---

(■)    **Discussion of activity**

Arranging tasks such as these efficiently is a personal matter, but here are some principles to consider. They may appear self-evident, but you may be surprised to see the extent to which you have or have not applied them in the activity.

Tasks which require concentration need periods of uninterrupted time and they are also best done at a time of day which suits the individual's metabolism. This is one's prime time, and it may be early in the morning or late at night, depending on the person. Tasks which rely significantly on what is in short-term memory need to be completed as soon as possible, and this is true irrespective of the detail of any notes taken at the time, because notes can never record everything and are often difficult to transcribe. Tasks which do not rely on concentration can be done at the same time as things such as talking to people or watching television.

In the activity, you may have felt that the most important aspect of the interview was that the concentration for it demanded no interruptions. If so, it would have been sensible to schedule it into a lengthy period of uninterrupted time – perhaps at home when other people in the family have gone to bed, or perhaps during a weekend when they are out, or perhaps when a room in the department is quiet. Alternatively or additionally, you may have felt that the concentration demanded your prime time. You may have felt that the most important aspect of the interview was that it had to be dealt with immediately while still fresh in your mind. If so, you would have scheduled it for immediately and moved other tasks accordingly.

Least concentration would be needed for sticking on the stamps. So it would be efficient to do this at a time when interruption is likely, or when you are likely to be tired or are watching television. Never waste precious prime time on such things.

Did you think of suggesting the meeting for a time which would least disrupt you? Perhaps in the middle of the day if you wanted to use it as a break; or perhaps at the beginning or end of the day if you wanted it to interfere as little as possible with a task requiring extended time. Timetabling to suit yourself is not selfish or self-centred, provided that the other person's preferences are also allowed for, and it is one of the most important aspects of time management.    ⬤

## Dealing with interruptions

Some people can work with interruptions, but most people, particularly as they get older, prefer to work without them. The following activity provides a stimulus for developing ways of dealing with interruptions.

 **Activity**

Is there a place to work where you won't be interrupted, such as at home when everyone is out, or in the library?

Is it reasonable to put a notice on a door somewhere giving a time when you will be available and requesting not to be disturbed until then?

Can you work in a room in the department, such as a laboratory or computer cluster room, out of hours so that no one else is there?

Can you let the phone ring when you are really busy or use an answerphone and call back at your convenience?

## Managing time at home with the family

Special difficulties arise when working at home and having to deal with interruptions from the family. It is natural for them to feel that

LIBRARY
EDUCATION CENTRE
PRINCESS ROYAL HOSPITAL

the home is a place for being together; it is not that they are unsympathetic or insensitive. Some people find the following tactics useful:

- At the outset of the research degree, negotiate an informal contract with partners, older children and other relatives about time
  commitments; their implications; and how long a period of time
  you expect the contract to have to last. (If you did not do this at
  the time, it is probably not too late to do it now.)
- Every weekend, or at some other convenient time, it is a good
  idea to go through your diary with your family, to agree what
  periods you can spend with them and when you ought to be
  working. Work periods are likely to increase considerably while
  writing up or finalizing the thesis, and sensitivity is needed on
  how and when to let the family know this.
- When you start a period of work at home, it can be helpful to
  role-play the 'joke' of saying a formal 'Goodbye, I'm going off to
  the office now' and a formal 'Hello, I've come back' when you are
  ready again for disturbances.

(■)   **Activity**

Can you adapt any of the above suggestions to fit your own circumstances?

### Keeping 'office hours' versus using the 'psychological moment'

As the adage about research being 99% perspiration suggests, research
certainly does involve long periods of routine work. Some research
students recommend keeping to 'office hours' during these periods,
to ensure a balance between work and social and leisure activities.

Often, however, the routine work needs to be sparked off by an
idea. Indeed, many research students say that they can go for days
without producing seemingly productive work; then an idea occurs
to them, together with immense enthusiasm for pursuing it. If they
can work on it then, they produce a great deal of high-quality work

very quickly. If, on the other hand, other commitments force them to delay for any reason, the moment seems to have gone, and the work, when it is eventually started, is slow and hard going. It is worth trying to recognize these 'psychological moments', and, if at all possible, letting them take over, even at the expense of other commitments and office hours.

## Keeping going for hours at a time

During some parts of a research degree, particularly while writing reports or finalizing the thesis, it is not unusual for research students to keep working at their books or their computer for 12 or more hours at a time. This can be due to the pressures of work and it can be due to pure delight and fascination. Do realize the dangers of sitting in front of a computer screen for long periods: eye strain, excessive tiredness, unknown effects on pregnant women, repetitive strain injury (see Box 9.2), etc. Humans need to take regular breaks.

---

**Box 9.2**  Repetitive Strain Injury

*Repetitive Strain Injury (RSI) is an acute inflammation of the muscles, ligaments and tendons and it's caused by performing the same physical task over and over again . . . Poor posture, sitting in a fixed position for too long, even stress and a tense body, can all combine to form RSI . . . The warning signs of RSI are aches or tingling in the fingers, wrists, elbows or shoulders. At the first sign of discomfort you should act. If you continue typing without improving your work habits, just hoping that the ache will go away, it may well develop into the shooting, burning pain that real sufferers know so well. In severe cases, they are hardly able to use their hands at all and a few end up disabled for life. Why some people and not others fall victim is all a bit of a mystery. But if RSI really gets you in its agonising grip, your doctor's first order will be to stop typing and possibly stop using your hands altogether for a time. Physiotherapy, ultrasound and even osteopathy can all help the sufferer. But it may take as long as six months before any activity is pain free . . . Prevention, as always, is easier than cure. For more advice contact The RSI Association, 152 High Street, Yiewsley, West Drayton, Middlesex, UB7 7BE.*

*(Prima, October 1994, p. 57)*

---

Cups of coffee and biscuits or chocolate bars often seem the obvious ways of justifying and filling them, but what many people find works better is some form of physical activity for five to ten minutes. It can be exercise or it can simply be one of the various tasks required for living, like washing up or making the bed. It can be a good idea to delay doing these so as to fill breaks, rather than rushing to get them all over before starting work.

Not infrequently, research students work far into the night. Only you can decide the extent to which it is advisable for you to go without sleep. It is not advisable as normal procedure, although it may be appropriate in certain circumstances.

## Matching your approach to your preferred learning style

Managing yourself can be made much more efficient if you get to know your own personal preferred learning style and then try to match your approach to it.

You may have already identified your preferred learning style. However, many new research students have never realized that there are alternative ways of setting about work. Consequently, they have never consciously analysed how they prefer to do it. Try the following activity.

(■)  **Activity**

When faced with a large task, do you find yourself breaking it down into smaller tasks and then starting somewhere with one small, well-defined task, and only after completing it going on to the next task? Or do you find yourself spending time trying to understand the full context of the large task before attempting any part of it? (If you are unsure, try to think of a concrete example, like designing an experiment for a particular purpose.)

Do you find yourself starting with the easiest parts of a task to get them out of the way, before concentrating on the harder ones, or do you prefer starting with the harder tasks?

When faced with new information, do you consciously consider whether your aim is simply to reproduce parts of it; to understand certain parts of it; or to understand as many implications and ramifications as possible?

---

## ⬛ Discussion of activity

There is no right or wrong learning style. It should be a matter for personal preference, dictated by the purpose behind the task. However, people who do not consciously bother to understand either their personal preferences or the range of possible learning styles, tend to assume implicitly that there is only one style, namely the one that they always use. Their work could be made much more efficient if they had a repertoire of learning styles that they could call upon according to the situation.

Letting a context emerge gradually by completing one task at a time is described as 'serialist' thinking. Needing to see the whole context before studying any part of it is described as 'holistic' thinking. The adage about 'not seeing the wood for the trees' is relevant here. It is normally used disparagingly to imply that someone cannot see clearly what they ought to be doing and where they ought to be going, and there is a lesson in this for research students, for whom it is important to be able to see the wood as well as the trees. Doing so requires holistic thinking, which will probably have to be cultivated, because early education normally trains children into serialist thinking at the expense of holistic thinking, in that high-priority subjects such as languages and mathematics require a step-by-step approach. Subjects which foster holistic thinking tend to have a lower priority. Art appreciation is an example because it can require the complete picture to be taken in at a glance before the detail is considered. A technique to foster holistic thinking is the use of mind maps, which are introduced in Chapter 16.

The intention to reproduce material without understanding it involves what is called a 'surface approach' to learning, and the intention to develop personal understanding involves what is called a 'deep approach'. It is not true that research students should always use the deep approach, although of course no academic work could progress with an entirely surface approach. Both approaches have their places, and what is important is to decide which approach to use in which circumstances and why. ⬛

## Using music to manage yourself

Some people work best with complete quiet. Others find that music can increase their efficiency. Most people know their musical preferences by the time they become research students. What they may not appreciate is that different types of music can be better for different types of work. Use the following activity as a basis for discussion with others, to see if they can make any suggestions about use of music.

 **Activity**

If you like to work with background music, what pieces or styles are your preferences for the following?

• Reading

• Writing

• Creative thought

• Routine administrative work

⬛ **Discussion of activity**

Some people find that certain routine administrative work, such as the sticking of stamps on envelopes mentioned earlier, can wind them up because it is only occupying part of their mind. Music can occupy the other part, and hence make the work more relaxing. But the music has to be the right sort (see Box 9.3).

---

**Box 9.3** Background music

This contribution on the use of background music for study is from a research student in music education at Roehampton Institute London.

*For many years music has been used in a variety of educational settings to enhance learning. Research in psychology has frequently delved into the effects of background music on human performance, but mostly with inconsistent results.*

*Personally I find that music does help with certain aspects of my studies as a research student, but other research students do not all find the same. In general, silence is preferred when reading an important article or book, and one of the research students here even puts in ear plugs to block out all auditory distractions! When involved in other activities the choice of background music depends on the sort of work being carried out and the mood of the individual concerned. The radio can give a constant train of music in the background, and the choice of station depends of course on the individual. Other research students report that they listen to a variety of stations, ranging from Classic FM to Virgin Radio, to Radio 4 and Radio 1. Personally I find that the talking in between the music is a distraction.*

*There is a widespread belief that 'classical' music is most stimulating for study. However, a recent short project carried out here at Roehampton had some interesting findings: musicians worked more effectively on a given task with atonal background music, whereas non-musicians were distracted by this and preferred tonal background music by Mozart.*

*Here are some personal observations:*

- *I prefer to listen to music that has no words. Otherwise I am distracted and want to sing along!*
- *The music needs to be something that I am indifferent to. If not, and if it is music that I don't know, then I want to stop and listen to it, and if it is something that I know well, I am distracted by associations.*
- *I feel it is best to listen to music that does not have extremes of tempo or volume. Otherwise it becomes distracting. (Haydn's Surprise Symphony is not to be recommended!)*

- *Music tapes can have advantages and disadvantages. On the one hand, turning the tape over is an interruption; on the other hand it can be a way of keeping track of time. For example, one can say to oneself that one wants to finish a certain task by the end of the tape.*
- *Working to music may actually be an aid to concentration as it can block out other distracting noises.*

*It is not possible to dictate music that necessarily helps people to work, because everyone has their own individual tastes and ways of working, but here are a few suggestions that work well for me and which other research students say work well for them.*

*For the 'over-stressed-need-to-relax' research students:*

- *Zen Shakuhachi. As Japanese music is my research area, I have to recommend this tape with enthusiasm! It is meditative music of the Japanese bamboo flute, available in the World Music section of any good record shop.*
- *Bushland Dreaming. This is Australian Nature Series 3 by Tony O'Connor, and others in the series are also good. They are available from the World Music section of any good record shop.*
- *Indonesian Gamelan. Also available from the World Music section of any good record shop.*
- *Pachelbel's Canon Compilation. A very relaxing tape of various ensembles playing this lovely tune.*
- *Classical Guitar. John Williams has many recordings of popular classics.*
- *Scriabin Piano Sonata No. 2. A favourite of mine.*
- *Medieval music. Available in any well-stocked record shop.*

*For the 'urge-to-be-busy' research students:*

- *Baroque or classical music features strongly. Romantic music such as late Beethoven has far too many contrasts which tend to be a distraction for study.*
- *Bach – Brandenburg Concertos.*
- *Vivaldi – Lute and Mandolin Concerto.*
- *Haydn Symphonies – plenty to choose from!*
- *Runrig (a Scottish Gaelic Band).*
- *Riverdance. (Irish traditional music such as this has a good beat to get one on the move!)*

*Of course these are only a few suggestions and no doubt most people will use a combination of silence, recordings and radio as a background for studying. It is a matter of individual choice.*

(Bernadette Wilkins, personal communication, 1995)

Playing taped music serves the purpose that the end of a tape forces people to realize how long they have been working and that it is time for a break, even if that break is simply changing the tape.

## Matching your methodology to suit your personal needs and preferences

There is usually some flexibility in designing a research programme, particularly where the precise formulation of the research problem grows out of choices made at the various stages of the research. So it makes sense to build in personal preferences, because doing what one likes aids efficiency. Use the following activity to set your mind thinking.

(■)   **Activity**

Give an approximate rating for how much the following modes of working appeal to you personally. Then discuss with people who know you well.

• Working alone


• Work involving being with or talking to people generally


• Work involving being with or talking to specific types of people


• Work involving long hours of private study


• Work involving making or using equipment


• Work which is primarily out of doors

- Work which is primarily of use to others

- Work which is primarily of personal fascination

- Work which involves travelling

---

(■)  **Discussion of activity**

Some or all of the above modes of working, and other modes as well, will be required to some extent in all research degrees, but research students usually have more freedom than they realize in terms of designing their work around the modes of working that are most enjoyable or fascinating to them personally. The freedom is most where the research students are working alone in a way where decisions about the direction of the work at any stage grow out of the findings of previous stages. The freedom is least where the research involves teamwork.

If you have flexibility and, for example, you happen to prefer working away from other people, it is perfectly possible to define a research problem and develop an appropriate methodology reinterpreting data which is entirely secondary (that is, already collected by other researchers and probably already published). Then contact with others will be kept to a minimum. If you happen to prefer working with people, out of doors or in any other particular situation, you should be able to design a research programme to maximize this.  (■)

## Fitting in teaching work

Research students are often offered teaching or laboratory demonstration work within their departments. This has the advantage of providing both money and experience, but care needs to be taken that it does not seriously detract from the business of the research degree. Some individuals find that a 'teaching session' overshadows the complete day because they work themselves up for it and then need time to unwind afterwards. If you do decide to take on teaching work, make sure that it suits your disposition and that you receive some suitable training. The National Postgraduate Committee has produced guidelines for the employment of postgraduate students as teachers which are referenced in the Further Reading section.

Teaching and laboratory demonstration work should be at your choice and never imposed.

## Maintaining a healthy lifestyle

Part of managing one's self must be to maintain a healthy lifestyle, giving attention to adequate and appropriate exercise and to healthy eating. This is particularly important for research students, who feel that things are getting on top of them. Dealing with this includes maintaining a balanced outlook by keeping physically fit.

According to a recent television programme (*The Lady Killers*, ITV, 16 August 1995, 10.40pm), long term, serious depression is readily avoidable and treatable on three levels, according to its severity: physical exercise, which releases natural therapeutic chemicals into the body; talking things over; and then – if these fail – taking drugs prescribed by a doctor. The dangers of taking drugs which are not prescribed by a doctor are well-known.

## Being realistic with yourself

It is too easy to be unrealistic about what it is reasonable or possible for you or anyone else to do in a given time. If you aim at too much, you will get fraught and disappointed when you fail to achieve. If you aim at too little, you will never complete the research degree. You have to get to know yourself, and then be firm with yourself while at the same time treating yourself with generosity and understanding.

# 10 TAKING RESPONSIBILITY FOR YOUR OWN PROGRESS

*The people who get on in this world are the people who get up and look for the circumstances they want, and if they can't find them, make them.*

(George Bernard Shaw, *Mrs Warren's Profession*, Act II)

## The importance of keeping on learning

There is a core of basic knowledge and basic research skills that all research students in any field will need, and you may be fortunate enough to belong to a department that is sufficiently large to provide this training on a formal basis. However, as your work progresses, its uniqueness should become increasingly clear. Consequently, your needs in terms of research skills and knowledge will be different from those of any other research student. Do not expect these needs to be satisfied without taking at least some of the initiative yourself. It is your responsibility, in negotiation with your supervisor, to take responsibility for satisfying your own needs. This chapter considers ways of going about it.

## Training in basic research skills

It is essential that you and all the other research students in the department are firmly grounded in the basic skills and strategies of research in the discipline. If you belong to a department that runs a programme of training for its research students, it is unlikely that you will have any serious gaps in this area. If you do not belong to such a department, you may like to use the activity below as a checklist to identify where you might need to top up.

## (■) Activity

The following is a list of topics which could be in an interdisciplinary core research training programme for research students. (It is not meant to be ideal or comprehensive!) Does it spark off ideas about any topic that you feel you ought to know more about? When doing this activity, do bear in mind that each discipline has its own vocabulary and its own way of looking at research, so some topics may require different names, and some topics may naturally fit within others.

- Designing a research project
- Conducting a literature search
- Ways of gathering data
- Ways of analysing data
- Developing academic discourse and constructing arguments and counter-arguments
- Writing the thesis
- Giving a seminar on one's work
- Giving a conference paper
- Writing a journal article
- Research paradigms
- Ethical issues
- Intellectual copyright
- Career planning

## (■) Discussion of activity

It is difficult to identify the boundary between basic training for research and learning about research on the job, which is an on-going activity with ever more to learn. Time is of the essence for research students, so they have to find a balance between, on the one hand, ensuring that their basic training is adequate and, on the other hand, not wasting time learning things they may never use. If the activity has stimulated the feeling that you really do need a particular aspect of basic research training, do ask your supervisor to recommend courses, books or someone to talk to.

There is also the issue that the meaning and scope of research training are interpreted differently from one field of study to another.

In the arts and humanities, it is widely assumed that once research students are trained in how to go about research, they can find out about various methods or techniques for themselves, should this become necessary. In the sciences, each research method tends to require a unique competence with specialized equipment; and research students often feel justified in demanding a wide range of experience of different methods, irrespective of their applicability to the research problem, so that they can quote this experience in job applications. ●

## Training in transferable skills

Many departments feel that they have a responsibility to train their research students in personal skills, also known as 'transferable skills', so as to give them the edge on other applicants for employment.

---

**Box 10.1**   The value of transferable skills

The Director of Planning and Communication of the Engineering and Physical Sciences Research Council offers views that many would consider generalizable to all disciplines:

*The PhD was originally envisaged to be training for the next generation of academics; yet only a small percentage of PhD graduates in science and engineering (certainly less than 20% overall) can expect to obtain faculty appointments. There must therefore be concern that the majority of PhD graduates in science and engineering, who may not remain in academia long term, may not be adequately equipped with the broad range of skills that will fit them for a variety of employment opportunities.*

*By the nature of their research projects, many PhD research students do acquire a vast range of transferable skills. Thus, for example, PhD graduates in 'big science' subjects such as particle physics and space research are sought after not so much for their specialist knowledge but because their research training provided the opportunity for them to work in multidisciplinary teams where they acquired a breadth of experience in team building, working to schedules and budgets, turning their hand to a range of technical and data analysis challenges, and so forth.*

(Clark, 1995, p. 101)

---

How much can be done in this area must depend on the time available and the nature of employment prospects. Completing the research degree must be the first priority.

There is no definitive list of transferable skills, because they are so interrelated. What follows is a checklist which you may like to peruse. It may set you thinking about opportunities to develop these skills that may even facilitate progress on your research.

- Presentation skills
- Interview techniques
- Planning, finance and business strategies
- Teamwork
- Leadership
- Personnel management

## Keeping up with your subject

Research students are expected to know what is regarded as 'all the basic and important literature in the field'. So you need to try to keep abreast with developments by reading core and closely related literature. The difficult balancing act is drawing a line between the core and the related. You don't have the time to read everything.

Research students also need to keep abreast with new developments by sitting in on various courses and seminars. However, this too is a matter of balancing the potential usefulness of the information with the time spent acquiring it. In an academic community it would be quite possible to spend all your time following only marginally related interests, and, fascinating as they may be, they cannot write a thesis for you.

## Networking and serendipity

As your work develops, you will probably find the need for research tools and techniques that you did not learn about in your basic training. They may be something that everyone knows the existence of, even if they do not know how to use them, such as statistics. On the other hand, they may be something that the staff in your department cannot be expected to know about. Then the only way to find out is to make a point of going out and meeting other researchers, talking to them, letting them know what you are doing – that is to say, networking and keeping your eyes and ears open, giving serendipity a chance. Box 10.2 gives an example of its usefulness.

**Box 10.2** The value of serendipity in research

Lewis Elton tells the story – which he admits dates him! – of how he first learnt about computers at a time when they were very new. He was giving a conference presentation in which he regretted that he could not follow up a particular approach because the calculations would be impossibly onerous. One of the participants came up to him afterwards and suggested that the mathematics would not be at all onerous if he used the new technique of computers and that he himself had a suitable program. Between them they did indeed use the computers and the program, and completed the work successfully.

## Using research seminars

Most departments run regular research seminars. In such seminars the discussion that takes place afterwards is as important as the content of the presentation. Although your first thought may be to doubt the value of attending a seminar where the topic is far removed from your own, your further thoughts should be very different unless you are very near the end of your work. There are four main reasons.

One reason for attending research seminars is that they are likely to be your only access to academic staff other than your supervisor. Not that these individuals will be objectively in any way superior to a supervisor, but they will have different ranges of experiences to call on and different ways of expressing themselves. You should learn a lot about what does and does not constitute good research by listening to their contributions to the discussion and then testing out your own input from their reactions.

A second reason for attending is to give yourself access to what is going on in different and related areas, in case you may need to link it to your own work (see Chapter 15).

A third reason for attending is to develop an appreciation of the research culture of your discipline.

A fourth reason for attending is to learn about how to give a seminar yourself.

A valid reason for not attending departmental research seminars is that they are so badly attended by others that it is not possible to gain the benefits outlined above. It may be possible, though, if you choose the right time and place so as not to cause offence, to have a word with the seminar organizer to suggest ways of boosting attendance, for example by moving the seminars to a different time of day.

# 11 COOPERATING WITH OTHERS FOR MUTUAL HELP AND SUPPORT

*No man is an Island.*

(John Donne, 'Meditation XVII',
*Devotions upon Emergent Occasions* (1624))

## The importance of mutual help and support

Although doing a research degree can mean a great deal of working in isolation, successful research students invariably rely heavily on the support of others – to suggest leads, to give informed judgements, to provide constructive criticism and to boost motivation. This chapter is about giving and receiving help and support from others: other research students; other academics; family and friends; and other professionals in the department, institution and elsewhere.

## The ethics of using help from other people

In an academic community, there is no shortage of ideas, and there is nothing inherently wrong in finding out about them and using them. It is accepted academic practice to acknowledge sources, but do realize that if you turn a lead into a significant part of your research degree, it is you and you alone who deserve the credit for recognizing its significance and developing it into something forceful and academically convincing. This is neither cheating nor any other form of misconduct. Box 11.1 gives an overview of what can constitute misconduct in research.

A good way of indicating that the work is essentially yours, though you had some help, is to acknowledge the help in an Acknowledgements section.

---

**Box 11.1** The nature of misconduct in research

Misconduct in research includes:

*(a) The fabrication of data: claiming results where none has been obtained.*

*(b) The falsification of data including changing records.*

*(c) Plagiarism, including the direct copying of textural material, the use of other people's data without acknowledgement and the use of ideas from other people without adequate attribution.*

*(d) Misleading ascription of authorship including the listing of authors without their permission, attributing work to others who have not in fact contributed in the research, and the lack of appropriate acknowledgement of work primarily produced by a research student/trainee or associate.*

*(e) Other practices that seriously deviate from those commonly accepted within the research community for proposing, conducting or reporting research.*

*(f) Intentional infringement of the institution's published code of conduct for the responsible conduct of research.*

*Misconduct does not include honest errors or honest differences in interpretation on judgements of data.*

*This list is not meant to be all inclusive.*
(Australian Vice-Chancellors's Committee, 1990, p. 5)

---

## The ethics of giving help to other people

Just as it is unethical to take other people's work and present it as your own, it is equally unethical for other people to take your work and present it as their own. Everyone has what is known as 'intellectual copyright' or 'intellectual property rights' on their own work. Most supervisors are entirely open and honest if they wish to use their students' work, either in their own publications or for commercial reasons, and they see to it that the student gets full credit and a fair share of any financial remuneration. You may, however, suspect that you are not being treated fairly in this respect. The law is complicated and keeps changing; so a good way forward might be to speak to an officer of the students' union in the first instance.

The Further Reading section lists a useful publication to structure your enquiries.

## Supporting and getting support from other research students

Research students in the same department or research group may be able to give advice and support relating specifically to the subject of your research. This should work both ways, in that you should be willing to give advice and support in return. Research students from other departments and other institutions can give advice and support of a more general nature. If you can build up a mutual support group with one or more research students, all of you will benefit. Such self-help or support groups can be large or small; formal or informal; ongoing or transient. In any of these forms, they can serve their members well.

## Getting support from academic staff

Other academics can be used in the same way as other research students: to suggest useful references or information on what is going on and leads to explore. However, academics are busy people and will not welcome being expected to spend time solving your problems. Also they have a professional duty towards their colleagues. So do not put them in the position of having to listen to what could be construed as criticism of how a supervisor supervises you. Also, if you want a formal consultation, do clear it with your supervisor first.

## Soliciting help from academics in other institutions

Most academics have stories to tell of receiving letters from research students they have never met, asking for general leads and information. Academics seldom look favourably on such requests. Firstly, they smack of the research students apparently trying to get someone else to do their work for them; and secondly, they show a lack of understanding of what research degrees ought to be about. General leads can, after all, be gathered from institutional libraries, and research degrees ought to be about research students processing ideas themselves and then following through the themes that develop.

Unfavourable reactions do not extend to requests for specific unpublished pieces of information in an academic's own published research area, where these are phrased in such a way as to show that research students have already done sufficient basic work themselves to recognize the significance of their requests. Then academics usually do what they can to help and their advice can be very valuable (see Box 11.2).

---

**Box 11.2** A definition of an expert

*[An expert is] someone who knows some of the worst mistakes that can be made in his subject, and how to avoid them.*
(Heisenberg, 1971, p. 210)

---

 **Activity**

---

On the basis of your reading, name a few national and international experts in your field.

Develop a few questions that you would ask each of them if you were to meet them. These should be questions that would further your work while not causing them irritation.

If this activity stimulates questions that would seem to be really worthwhile following up, think about how you might establish contact.

## Getting support from family and friends

If you are a mature student living with your family, you will realize that they will have much to put up with while you are working for a research degree. You may work late into the night, or over weekends, or at other times that might be considered as 'belonging' to them. You may be short of money and they may have to go without. You may be preoccupied for much of the time. Tell them what to expect from the outset, negotiate ways of meeting their needs as well as yours, and get their support.

If your family and friends have also studied for a research degree, you may also be able to enlist their help in the same way as with academics and fellow research students. They do not need to have a background in the same subject. If you talk about your work, they can come to know it almost as well as you do. They can react by pointing out logical inconsistencies and they can also suggest ideas and new directions.

## Giving advice, feedback and criticism

Helping others will involve giving them advice, feedback and criticism on their work. Before going ahead with it, do make sure that they actually want it, and do not proceed otherwise. Try to understand their insecurity and put them at ease by starting with a comment about something you like – you will always be able to find something if you set your mind to it. Before moving to anything critical, suggest extenuating circumstances if this seems appropriate, and ask how they would do it differently another time. Propose realistic ways forward. Make your suggestions for consideration, not as unequivocal statements of what must be done. Take the attitude that you can comment constructively because you are not so close to the work, not because you are in any way superior. Close with good wishes and offers of future help.

If you do not have time to prepare feedback properly, it is usually safest not to give it at all. It is unfair to give weak, ill-considered platitudes which are of no help, or to upset people by giving feedback destructively. Being able to give constructive, acceptable feedback takes time, but is worth working at. It is a hallmark of academic ability and will serve you well along any career path which involves working with people.

## Receiving advice, feedback and criticism

Chapter 6 gave advice on receiving advice, feedback and criticism from your supervisor. Receiving it from others is very similar. They will want you to take the trouble to understand what they are saying; will hope that you are pleased about it; and will want you to take time to consider it. So the best thing to do is simply to thank the person, to seek clarification if necessary and then to say that you will go away and do some thinking. It is seldom worth launching into a justification of why what they say may be inappropriate. If you do, you may irritate them and probably prevent them from giving further help in future. It is quite in order not to accept the advice, feedback or criticism exactly as it stands, because only you know all the ramifications for your own work and situation. Only when you have taken time to consider can you decide how much to accept, reject or adapt. If the advice is substantial and you do accept it, formal acknowledgment is warranted.

Occasionally people give feedback which seems designed only to make themselves feel superior by denigrating others. This can be because the individuals concerned have been caught at a bad moment, in which case they usually apologize later. People who give destructive feedback as a norm invariably lose the respect of those around them. If you find that you are receiving destructive criticism on a regular basis, stay polite and take whatever steps are necessary to put an end to it.

# 12 PRODUCING REPORTS

*Woolly writing is frequently a reflection of woolly thinking, and a student who has trained himself to write clearly will soon discover that a problem of expression often arises from a lack of understanding, whereas a student who writes poor English can write rubbish without even realising it.*
(Science and Engineering Research Council, 1992, p. 16)

## The importance of reports in a research degree programme

In a research programme, reports may have to be produced for various reasons. At one extreme is the informal and private report that research students may choose to write as part of their own records, to provide an overview of how the work is progressing. At the other extreme are formal reports which may be required by the department at specified stages of the research programme to maintain or update registration and as part of quality assurance procedures. Between these extremes are less formal reports required by supervisors as part of general supervisory practice.

Report writing may benefit you in any of the following ways, although the relative importance of each will change as the programme of work progresses:

- to see whether you are on target with your work, so that any problems can be spotted in time to be attended to;
- to provide an opportunity for you to reflect on progress, consolidate arguments and identify any gaps in knowledge, data or methodology;
- to help you to develop an appreciation of standards and hence to learn to monitor your own progress;
- to provide practice in academic report writing and academic discourse, so that any additional training which may be necessary in this respect can be supplied at an early stage;

- to form a basis, in due course, for your thesis and possibly a journal article.

Although the suggestions in this chapter are general and may not necessarily be appropriate for all fields of study, they should never-theless stimulate your own thinking and indicate topics for discus-sion with your supervisor.

## Developing the content of a report

The content of a report must depend on its purpose. For most fields of study, the content of early informal reports probably ought to be such as to review progress to date in the light of one or more research questions or themes of the research problem or topic – possibly as stated in the original research proposal – and to identify a plan of action for the next phase of the work.

Reviewing progress to date is not merely a matter of showing what tasks you have done, although this will come into it. Rather, you should make a case that what you have done has been thoughtful, directed and competent. You should probably include the following, presented where possible as a substantiated argument rather than as a straight description:

- how you have defined or developed the research question(s), topic(s) or theme(s) with which the report is concerned;
- how you are developing your research methodology, stressing how it is appropriate;
- how you expect to ensure that you will collect appropriate data which is convincing for its purpose;
- how you are using the literature;
- how you are dealing, where necessary, with subjectivity;
- how far you have got;
- problems or potential problems which you would like to flag up;
- general reflections (these should be relevant, not just padding, and the nature of what is required is likely to vary considerably from one discipline to another).

As time progresses and your work moves on, the emphasis should change to include what you have done as well as what you intend to do.

For a formal report which specifies headings or sections, it is prob-ably a good idea to start by drafting brief notes along the above lines and then to edit them together, in negotiation with your super-visor. Incidentally, any headings which may appear bureaucratic or irrelevant could be intended to provide the institution with data for its quality assurance procedures.

## Structuring the report

Reports should be structured with a coherence that can only emerge from hindsight, and if this means writing little or nothing about something that occupied a great deal of time, so be it. No report should be a list of activities in chronological order. It should have a clear purpose and should be structured to make the case for something, such as the next stage of work or a conclusion to a previous piece of work.

To achieve a clear structure, it is helpful to think in terms of the need for a storyline, and a good way to demonstrate the storyline and so aid thinking about structuring is to make the title and major and minor headings sufficiently detailed that they tell the story. Then shortcomings in structure are immediately obvious from the contents list and can be duly attended to.

(■)  **Activity**

Look at some reports or journal articles in your own field; if contents lists are not supplied, make them by scanning the texts.

The chances are strong that the contents lists could be improved so as to communicate the storyline better. Make some suggestions.

(■)  **Discussion of activity**

A good way of enabling contents lists to communicate storylines is to attach such words as 'identifying', 'preparing', 'using', 'analysing' to the main topic of the title, section or sub-section.

You would be well advised to keep an up-to-date contents list to hand while writing your reports. It is in these that lack of coherence is likely to show first, and if you spot and deal with it early, you avoid wasting time producing text that will have to be discarded later.

In some discipline areas it would be neither acceptable nor normal practice for academic writing to have headings, so do use your judgement.  ⬛

## Constructing the introductory paragraph as an orientation

Readers of reports need to be orientated to what the report is about, and how it is structured. There is a presentational technique for achieving this. The first step is to write a few keywords or some notes under each of the following headings:

- Setting the scene for the report, i.e. the general area(s) that the report considers.
- The gap in knowledge or understanding which the report addresses.
- How the report fills the gap.
- A brief overview of what is in the report.

Then the notes are edited together to form the introductory paragraph.

⬛  **Activity**

---

Assume that you are about to write the introduction to a report on a piece of work you have been doing recently. Write a few keywords or some notes under each of the above headings and then edit them together into an introductory paragraph.

---

## Constructing the final paragraph for effective closure

The concluding paragraph of a report should serve as an effective closure. The technique for doing this starts with writing a few keywords or some notes under each of the following headings:

- What the report has done.
- What new questions the report has identified.
- How you will deal with these new questions or how you hope that others might do so.

Then the notes are edited together into the concluding paragraph.

(■)   **Activity**

_____

Imagine that you are about to write the concluding paragraph to the report of the previous activity. Write a few keywords or some notes under each of the above headings and then edit them together into a concluding paragraph.

_____

## Incorporating references to the literature

Literature should be used to substantiate and carry forward an argument; it should never be a catalogue of everything you could find that might seem remotely relevant to a topic. However, where seminal works in the general area are not directly relevant, you would be unwise to omit them. Try instead to find a way of bringing them in, possibly in terms of what they do not do, thus making a case for work that still needs to be done.

The following activity illustrates the use of literature to carry an argument forward.

● **Activity**

---

The following are two alternative versions of a paragraph from a report. Comment on the good, bad and interesting aspects of each.

1  Brown (1991) reports on a study based on questionnaires to explore the feelings of teachers in Poppleton School about using self-study materials to teach school children, but she does not tease out mathematics from the other subjects taught in the school. Smith (1992) uses interview techniques to elicit how a sample of mathematics lecturers in several universities feel about using self-study materials. No studies appear to be reported in the literature about the reactions from school teachers to using self-instructional materials for teaching mathematics to school children, although Jones (1939) argues strongly for the need for such studies if the teaching of mathematics in schools is to be made more efficient. This article reports on work which addresses this omission.

2  Questionnaires have been used to explore the reactions of teachers to using self-study materials to teach school children (Brown 1991). Interviews have been used with mathematics lecturers in several universities (Smith 1992). There is a need for studies with mathematics school teachers if the teaching of mathematics in schools is to be made more efficient (Jones 1939). This article reports on work which addresses this need.

**Discussion of activity**

The following are some of the issues that you may have considered.

Words such as 'reported' and 'argued', as used in the first version, inspire confidence that the writer has read and understood the literature. In contrast, the second version leaves the reader in ignorance of the nature of the quoted work or its conclusions, and so gives the impression that the writer could be quoting secondary literature without having ever read or understood the primary literature.

The first version reinforces the feeling of conviction that its writer is intimately familiar with the referenced work because the sex of the workers is shown to be known.

The first version also gives what is absent from the literature as an argument for the reported work. This adds to the conviction that the writer has a good grasp of relevant literature and is using it to substantiate argument.

You may have found areas where you felt that the second version was better than the first, for example, in its brevity. You will probably also have identified further interesting differences between the alternative paragraphs. ■

## Using appendices

Different disciplines have different norms about the use of appendices. A view at one extreme is that the main text of a report should be for making a substantiated case for something, and anything that interrupts the flow of the argument, such as tables of data, should be placed in an appendix and merely referred to in the text. A view at the other extreme is that if material is worthy of a place in a report, it should be in the main text.

■ **Activity**

Ask around in the department and look at some reports and theses to find out normal practices for the use of appendices.

## Developing an academic writing style

In some fields of study, by the time research students come to write a report, they will be thoroughly familiar with the accepted style of academic writing and academic argument in the discipline. This is not the case in all fields of study. If you feel ill prepared for academic writing, work with your supervisor, other research students or, if English is not your first language, the institutional language centre.

Academic writing relies on coherence, argument and precise meanings of terms. Other issues to consider are whether it is normal in your discipline to:

- write discursively or to use section headings and bullet points to break up the text and orientate the reader;
- use the active or the passive voice for reporting your own involvement, e.g. 'I did something' or 'something was done' (Box 12.1 illustrates some pros and cons);

---

**Box 12.1** Use of active and passive voices in academic writing

*In some subject areas, the use of the active voice in academic writing is regarded as unacceptable because it would indicate subjectivity and lack of modesty. Yet consider the following:*

*'The liquid was evaporated.'*

*Which of the following might it mean?*

- *I heated the liquid as part of my work.*
- *Someone else did this part of the work for me.*
- *The liquid evaporated naturally over time without anyone doing anything to make it happen.*

*How far do you think it reasonable that academic writing which is supposed to be unambiguous should not permit clarification through use of the active voice?*

(Author's workshop exercise)

---

- use the past tense or the timeless present (the first version of the paragraph in the last but one activity is written in the 'timeless' present to imply that the work is as valid now as when it was done);
- use long and complex sentences (see the extract in Box 12.2).

**Box 12.2**   The fog factor – a guide to clear writing

*We are often told to use short words and write clearly. A helpful device here is the 'fog factor'.*

*For this, we count the words of three or more syllables and the number of sentences on about half a page of writing. (I count the long words in my head and the sentences on my fingers.) We then divide the number of long words by the number of sentences.*

*A piece with a fog factor of 2 or 3 remains easy to read. If the count goes up to 4 or 5, it becomes heavy going. Yet academic and technical writing often averages 6 to 8 long words per sentence and sometimes more than 10. Long words strain our short-term memory. They make it difficult to remember how a sentence started by the time we reach the end.*

*Good novelists cope with basics like life and death on a fog factor of less than 1. But in technical writing, we are handicapped. We need long jargon words like statistics, regression or correlation coefficient – they can be a useful shorthand if used often enough to be worth learning . . .*

*The definition of the fog factor is not watertight. Are there two syllables in 'ratio' or three? What about names, numbers and abbreviations? . . . Splitting a sentence in two will halve its fog factor . . . Not all sentences should however be short. That would make for too abrupt a style. But long sentences should be there for a reason, such as giving a qualification or illustration before the reader is allowed to stop and think.*

(Ehrenberg, 1982)

(■)   **Activity**

---

Select some theses or research articles in your subject area and examine the writing style.

If you are at all uncertain on any aspects of the style, discuss with your supervisor, other research students or the institutional language centre in advance of doing any of your own writing.

---

## Further advice on writing

Writing a report can seldom be done in a single attempt; it is generally a matter of progressively refining one section in the light of another. This cannot be done quickly, and most people who are new to it underestimate the time it takes. It is probably best to do your own typing on a word processor so that you can make revisions easily as they occur to you.

The early emphasis should be on producing a coherent whole. It is a waste of time to spend hours refining style, if what is written is likely to be discarded – although of course there is a balance to be struck. No one can develop coherence in meaning if the style is too rough. Don't worry too much about style or typing/spelling errors early on; just keep on, to develop a coherent piece of writing.

All writing is improved by the 'drawer treatment' – putting it away in a drawer (or somewhere else) and coming back to it after an intervening time in which you have been concentrating on something else, preferably after at least a few days. Then, coming fresh to what you have written, you can go into an editorial mode and tidy up the writing.

Throughout the writing, be meticulous about keeping backups! It is false economy to save money on floppy disks. Have a plentiful supply of these, and keep backups by date of several previous versions as well as the latest version. There are two reasons for doing this. Firstly, you may want to refer to what you wrote some time ago; and secondly, it is all too easy to overwrite a file on hard disk and then copy it on to a backup floppy before realizing that you have lost your backup as well as the current file – then having a backup of a previous version on another floppy is a life-saver.

## Using reports to get feedback and advice

If you are to get maximum benefit from your reports, it is important to get feedback on them. This may be done informally during the process of refining them with your supervisor, or it may be done formally in the light of a completed report. Either way, it needs to be done. Use the activity below as a checklist.

(■) **Activity**

Make sure that, either formally or informally, you receive feedback on your report which covers the following issues:

- Am I on target as far as expected progress is concerned, or are there any problems that ought to be addressed now?

- Am I reading adequately and demonstrating acceptable standards in my work?

- Am I reflecting sufficiently thoughtfully on my work?

- Is my writing style acceptable?

---

(■)  **Discussion of activity**

You should discuss with your supervisor how 'reflecting sufficiently thoughtfully' could be interpreted in your field of study, and what your particular needs are in this respect. For example, you may need to spot more effectively where, how and why others might argue differently from you, to acknowledge and explore this and then modify your own case accordingly; you may need to consider implications of your work more deeply; you may need to give your writing more of a 'drawer treatment' so that others do not have to spend unnecessary time and effort trying to understand it. Maybe some other form of thoughtful reflection is what you need.

Reports are crucial for the success of your research programme, and they will almost certainly form a basis for your thesis. It is in your interests to get them as right as you can and then take on board all the feedback that they generate.  (■)

# 13 GIVING PRESENTATIONS ON YOUR WORK

*The communication of the results of research is an integral part of the research process, which is incomplete and ineffective if findings are not made available to others.*

(Engineering and Physical Sciences Research Council, 1995, p. 9/1)

## The importance of giving presentations on your work

It is important for research students to be able to give confident and effective presentations on their work. Some departments require it as part of formal progress monitoring and others offer it as part of their training and support for research students. From your own point of view, giving a presentation on your work forces you to structure and evaluate it, which in turn enables you to spot, and hence remedy, flaws in arguments and to identify new ways forward. It also enables you to get feedback from others on what you have done so far and to benefit from their advice about what you might do in future, in terms of new lines of exploration, more appropriate tools or techniques and helpful literature.

Presenting to an audience is a large subject, and this chapter can only touch on those areas that seem to be of particular concern to research students. If you would like further information, there is no shortage of advice on the subject (see the Further Reading section). If you are already a fairly experienced presenter from your undergraduate or taught masters degree work, you may choose only to scan this chapter for revision purposes.

## Deciding on the purposes of your presentation

A presentation may have a variety of purposes, and before you do any serious preparation for one, you should identify yours and prioritize them. Some possibilities include:

- to show what you have achieved so far;
- to get advice and feedback from the audience;
- to provide a forum where everyone can learn and mutually support one another; and
- to contribute to assessment or monitoring procedures.

The relative priorities of each must depend on circumstances.

For formal monitoring purposes or for an information seminar near or after completion of the research programme, the priority should be to show what has been achieved and to provide a forum where everyone can learn from the speaker and from other participants. Even at this stage, though, where you could be forgiven for regarding the work as complete, it would be inappropriate not to incorporate getting advice and feedback from the audience. After all, further work can always still be done, even if not by you or for this particular research degree.

For a departmental seminar that is not part of a formal monitoring process, you would need to discuss purposes with your supervisor or the seminar organizer. It is likely that the emphasis ought to be on getting advice and feedback.

(■) **Activity**

Imagine that you are between six months and two years into your research and that you are going to give a seminar on it to the other research students and academics in the department.

Rate the relative importance of each of the following purposes for the seminar:

- To show what you have achieved so far
- To get help, advice and feedback
- To provide a forum for mutual help and support
- To contribute to assessment or monitoring processes

List several areas where you would like help, advice or feedback.

---

(■) **Discussion of activity**

Your rating of the relative importance of each of the purposes must depend on the situation and on the outcomes of discussion with your supervisor.

As far as the areas where you want help are concerned, you will not impress if they are such that you could help yourself given a few hours in the library or a few minutes with your supervisor. Neither will you impress if they are areas which might result in your supervisor seeming to be put down because he or she could have helped if only you had asked, without calling on the rest of the department. Including such areas could easily alienate people. The areas where you want help should link in some way to research methodology, research procedure, scholarship, argument or originality. There should not be too many of them, and it may be sensible to stick to only one. (■)

## Developing the content of the presentation

For all but the most experienced of seminar presenters, time usually passes much more quickly than expected. The difficulty is compounded because enough time ought to be left for audience participation afterwards. Many people would say that this ought to be as long again as the actual presentation. Therefore, when you come to prepare your seminar, you have to overcome the natural tendency to prepare too much material. You should think carefully about how much of your work needs to be described and explained for your particular purposes. It is good advice to present no more than a minimum of background material and not to give details that your audience has a right to expect that you can be trusted to have handled competently on your own.

The following are helpful starting points for thinking about what to put into the seminar:

- the purposes of the seminar;
- the purpose of the work on which the seminar will report;
- what has been achieved so far;
- options for ways forward, and their apparent advantages and disadvantages as you perceive them at the moment;
- what is likely to interest the audience.

It is a good idea to mark some of your topics as less important than others, so that you can leave them out if time catches up with you on the day. Similarly it is worth preparing some additional material, just in case you under-run. Also prepare and refer to points that the audience might like to raise during the discussion, and plan answers to likely questions.

## (■) Activity

Develop the content of the seminar that you thought about in the last activity, using, if you like, the ideas in the above section as starting points.

## Structuring the material

Once you have developed what to put into the presentation, it then has to be put into a logical sequence, under suitable headings. This logical sequence should be such that there are coherent themes running through. If one of these happens to be chronological, it should be coincidental. Often coherent themes can only be identified with hindsight.

### ⬛ Activity

---

Arrange the content of your seminar into a logical sequence.

Estimate how long it might take to present this material. This can only be a rough estimation, and will have to be readdressed from time to time as preparation continues. Cut the material down as necessary, but keep some in reserve in case of under-running.

---

### Developing visual aids

Handouts and transparencies for use with an overhead projector help the audience to follow the seminar and add to the professionalism of the presentation. They can take a long time to prepare well; so it is a good idea to sketch them out roughly in draft form on cheap paper, and then practise the presentation on the basis of the drafts. Produce the final-quality copies only once you are sure that the drafts are right.

The easiest and cheapest way to produce quality transparencies is to design them with a word processor, print them on to paper and then photocopy on to acetate. Some printers may print directly on to acetate, but the quality can be unreliable. Less professional, but none the less effective transparencies can be produced by writing with appropriate pens directly on to acetate sheets. (The types of acetate for these two purposes are different; so make sure you use the right sort.) The size of the lettering should be such that it can be read easily if the paper or the acetate sheet is propped up about a metre and a half from the eye, and this has implications for the amount of material that can be fitted in. If you want to include a diagram or a table that does not satisfy this test, make it into a handout as well as a transparency. Then the audience can read it from their own printed sheet while you point to the relevant parts of the transparency.

There is a balance to be struck between too many and too few visual aids: too many can be perceived as patronizing to a mature and intelligent audience, whereas too few will make the seminar difficult to follow. A general guideline is not to have more than one transparency or slide every few minutes.

It is worth remembering that people usually like to have some sheets of paper to take away from a seminar as an *aide-mémoire*.

The preparation and use of visual aids is a large topic. For further information, see the Further Reading section.

## Rehearsing and refining the presentation

If you get the chance, visit the seminar or lecture room sometime in advance to get a feel for what it will be like standing in front – addressing people at the back and using equipment like the overhead projector. There may be the option of using other equipment, such as a microphone, a slide projector, video playback equipment, and lighting and blind controls. If you decide to use any of these, you need to find out how to manage them yourself, or how to signal directions to a technician. Most audiences will be irritated if you waste time during the presentation finding out how to use the overhead projector or waiting while someone fetches something.

Rehearse the presentation in private to check that the timing is about right. Some people find it helpful to keep a clock or watch on the table in front of them. Inexperienced presenters find timing worrying, but there are ways of dealing confidently with it. If you find that you are over-running, never speed up to cram everything in and do not shorten discussion time. Instead, simply say what, if time had permitted, you would have spoken about. If you find that you are seriously under-running, include the extra material that you planned for just such a contingency. If you are only marginally under-running, simply finish early. No one will mind extra discussion time or even leaving early.

Practise sounding enthusiastic. If you are not interested in your work, no one else is likely to be. You may find it helpful to practise the seminar in front of someone who can provide constructive help, such as a member of your family or another research student. Do be open to their advice. If they spot a lack of consistency or an error, the chances are that they will be right and that the reason why you did not spot it yourself was not that it was not important, but that you are so familiar with your own work.

Other things to consider when you rehearse include whether you can be heard properly; whether to stand or sit; what clothes are appropriate; and body language to suggest the right degree of confidence. It seldom gives a good impression to read directly from a script, so you have to experiment with the form of notes that enables you to feel most comfortable. Some people find that the prompts on transparencies are enough; others like to make notes on cards.

If you feel nervous, it can help to learn the opening couple of sentences by rote and then ad lib from there. Think also about how to respond to questions that you will not be able to answer. It is usually best to admit it and ask if anyone else in the audience can help.

It may be useful to ask someone to come prepared to take notes on comments and advice from the audience, as it will be difficult for you to concentrate fully on these while also attending to the actual presentation.

Finally, find out at what stage your supervisor wishes to be involved in the preparation of your seminar. Never present it without at least giving him or her the opportunity to comment first.

## Drumming up attendance for a seminar

If a major purpose of giving a departmental seminar is to get advice and feedback, it is important that the audience should contain people who have the background and experience to give informed reactions. This usually means other academic staff. They are inevitably busy people, so it may be worth making a point of personally and individually asking them to attend. Even if they do not make particularly helpful comments at the seminar itself, they will get to know your work, and may therefore be able to pass on any useful tips which come their way later.

## Giving a conference presentation

Your supervisor will suggest that you give a presentation at a conference only when you are far enough into your work to have some meaningful results, and he or she should certainly tutor you to make sure that you are a credit to the department. So only a few words are in order here. A conference presentation is not the same as an internal seminar presentation, although it is similar to a presentation at a seminar for external participants. The purpose is different. Also time will be a much greater constraint.

The purpose of a conference presentation varies from one field of study to another, so check with your supervisor. It may be to put down a marker in the national or international academic community that it is you who are doing a specific piece of work, and that you are making good progress with it. A journal is the place for presenting completed work. Ideally, the conference presentation will result in publishers or other workers in related fields speaking or writing to you later, to follow up on your work. So all you need to present is what you are doing, why it is so important or interesting, how far you have got, what your results are so far, what they mean to you, and where you intend to go next. Describe your research methods briefly, but do not delve into the difficulties unless they are likely to be of significant interest to others. It is important that visual aids and handouts be very clear because you will want to convince your audience that you are someone to be taken seriously. Many a conference participant has been put off by transparencies that could not be read from the back of the room and by the presentation of too much material.

Since work is often publicized at conferences before it is formally published, conferences are good places to get information to keep ahead of the field and to find out who is heading what work in your general area. You may even meet your future examiners.

## Giving other types of presentation

Research students may find themselves giving presentations other than seminars or conference papers. Most likely would be presentations to prospective employers or funding agents and on departmental open days for next year's research students. The advice in this chapter can readily be adapted for such alternative presentations.

# 14 LANDMARKS, HURDLES, AND TRANSFERRING FROM MPhil TO PhD

> *Landmarks and feedback provide emotional security and remove ambiguity and doubt.*
>
> (Mathias and Gale, 1991, p. 9)

## The rationale for frameworks of progress checks

Most departments have a framework of formal and regular procedures to monitor and assess the progress of their research students. It enables them to see whether the research students are on target, so that if any problems exist, they can be spotted in time and attended to; it provides a formalized opportunity for research students to reflect on their progress, consolidate their arguments and identify any gaps in knowledge, data or methodology; and it helps research students to develop an appreciation of standards, to enable them better to monitor their own progress.

Different departments have different frameworks, not only because the institution may give them autonomy in this respect, but also because the requirements of different disciplines often vary considerably. A component which is common to most fields of study, is widespread across institutions in the United Kingdom and is particularly significant and meaningful is the process which transfers or upgrades registration to doctoral status. Other countries have similar procedures, such as probationary periods of various kinds, after which registration for the doctoral degree can be confirmed.

The straightforward path through all these procedures depends on knowing the administrative requirements; being competent as a researcher; and being able to produce credible documentation to justify oneself. In addition, transfer from MPhil to PhD also requires attention to the concepts of 'originality', 'significance' and 'independence'.

## Ascertaining the departmental framework of progress checks

Institutions may or may not impose specific procedures on departments for monitoring their research students' progress. Where they do not, it is becoming increasingly common, with the advent of institutional quality assurance and quality audit, for an institution to want to know what procedures a department has designed for itself. You need to find out first what these are, as formalized in official departmental and – where applicable – institutional documents, and second how they are interpreted in practice, as seen through the eyes of supervisors and other research students. Use the activity below as a checklist.

(■)  Activity

In each of the following categories, what are the formal departmental procedures for monitoring the progress of research students? Where procedures are absent or ambiguous, how are they normally interpreted, and how flexible are they?

• When and how often do the progress-monitoring events take place?

• What are the requirements from research students? For example:

– Writing a report or proposal of some sort. What precisely?

– Presenting a seminar

– Attendance at departmental meetings/seminars

– Submitting a paper to a refereed journal

• What are the requirements from the supervisors or from other academics?

• To whom should written material be submitted?

• To whom does it go for assessment?

---

(■) **Discussion of activity**

All monitoring procedures normally include writing some sort of report, although length and format will vary considerably from one department or institution to another and from one field of study to another. Chapter 12 gives some general advice on writing reports, and parts of Chapter 18 on writing theses may also be helpful. Monitoring procedures may also include giving a seminar; Chapter 13 offers advice.

Some departments hope that, as a landmark of progress, research students may submit an article or paper on their research to a refereed journal, perhaps sometime during their second or third year. Whether or not this is required should depend on the progress of the research and the time commitments of supervisors and research students. Where it is possible, it has the advantage of focusing the mind, as well as adding to the very important publications record of the department. If you do write a paper, your supervisor will almost certainly advise and will probably be a joint author.     (■)

## Transferring from MPhil to PhD

It is widespread practice in the United Kingdom for research students to register for an MPhil degree, and then, in time, if they wish and if the work is shown to be worthy, to transfer or upgrade registration to a PhD, backdated to the start of the MPhil. What this worthiness entails is well known in general terms (see Box 14.1),

---

**Box 14.1**   The distinction between an MPhil and PhD

*Subject to the institution's regulations, an MPhil thesis should be either a record of original work or an ordered and critical exposition of existing knowledge in any field. A PhD thesis must form a distinct contribution to the knowledge of the subject and afford evidence of originality, shown by the discovery of new facts or by the exercise of independent critical power.*

(National Postgraduate Committee, 1995, p. 3)

---

although interpretation differs considerably from one discipline to another. Ongoing discussion with supervisors and other academics is essential for arriving at an understanding of ranges of interpretation in your own field. Chapter 15 provides some general ideas.

Institutions do not necessarily impose rigorous or detailed upgrading procedures on departments. A department may have its own, which have been developed over time and in the light of experience and the needs of the discipline, and which may be quite different from those in other departments. Irrespective of what these procedures are, the institution usually accepts them. However, each research student's upgrade normally needs to be ratified individually by the institution, although this tends to be a formality. So, essentially, what research students have to do in order to upgrade is to satisfy the requirements of their departments, which may or may not be rigorous or formalized.

A first step is to find out what the procedures and requirements are, as laid out in official departmental or institutional documentation, and as normally interpreted in practice. Use the activity below as a checklist.

◉   **Activity**

---

In terms of each of the following, what are the formal procedures for transferring from MPhil to PhD in your department? Where they are absent or ambiguous, how are they normally interpreted, and how flexible are they?

• When is the earliest (i.e. how soon after you have registered for the MPhil) and the latest (i.e. how near to the anticipated completion date) that you can submit your upgrading documentation?

• What precisely is your upgrading document expected to show?

• Are there any formal requirements for the upgrading document, in terms, for example, of:

  – length?

  – section headings?

  – appendices?

• To whom should the upgrading document be submitted?

• To whom does the upgrading document go for consideration?

• What other requirements are there, if any? For example:

  – presenting a seminar

  – attendance at departmental meetings/seminars

  – testimonials from others

• What are the procedures by which the institution ratifies the decision to upgrade registration?

---

 **Discussion of activity**

Although departments vary considerably in terms of their requirements, the chances are strong that any upgrading document will be expected to do three things:

- review progress to date in the light of the original research proposal;
- identify one or more strands in the next stage of the work which show originality, significance and independence;
- develop a plan of action to complete the work to PhD standard.

Each of these is considered below.

## The upgrading document: reviewing progress to date

Reviewing progress to date is not primarily a matter of how you have spent your time, although this may be required by some departments. The emphasis should be on showing that what you have done has been thoughtful and competent. The following should probably be included, presented as far as possible as a substantiated argument rather than as straight description, with literature referenced fully and in the manner which is the norm for your discipline:

- How you defined the research topic or problem, taking your original proposal as the starting point.
- How you have developed your research methodology so far, from the originally defined research topic or problem.
- How you have ensured that you have collected data which is appropriate and convincing for its purpose.
- How you have used literature.
- How you have dealt with any problems and constraints.
- How far you have got.

Most of this should come out of previous reports and records. If much of it is new, you were probably not writing enough as you went along.

## The upgrading document: focusing on originality, significance and independence

By the time you come to upgrade, you should, in principle, have already been giving considerable thought over a lengthy period to how the next stage of your work is going to demonstrate originality, significance and independence. However, for research students working on certain science-based projects, this can be little more than a formality – something which academics in other fields tend to regret! It happens where research students are working as part of a team on a larger project, funded on a project grant, and possibly using unique equipment. The originality then comes from necessarily breaking new ground since no one else has that particular type of access to the equipment – although there can be worries that someone might be doing something somewhat similar somewhere else in the world, and might pip them at the post. The significance is built in, as the grant-giving body was prepared to fund the work. Independence, however, can be an issue, and research students in this position should, from the start, keep careful records to show which parts of the team's work and achievements are theirs.

In many fields of study, particularly the social sciences and the humanities, upgrading is far from a formality, and research students will need to have pondered hard and long on original and significant directions for the next stage of their work. This is where Chapters 15 and 16 should help. Independence is likely to be less of an issue because of the nature and relative isolation of the work; and whether or not significance is an issue can depend on making a case for the value of knowledge in its own right. Fortunately, students seldom need to worry about being pipped at the post, because of the uniqueness of their work. Even if something similar is published near the completion of the thesis, they can always produce a critique of it in the light of their own work.

The chances are that the emphasis of the new work will be on narrowing down the focus, rather than opening it up. The adage in Box 14.2, although intentionally flippant, does carry more than an element of truth.

---

**Box 14.2** At last! A definition of a PhD

Here is a flippant adage which carries more than an element of truth.

*A PhD is about finding out more and more about less and less until one eventually knows everything about nothing.*

(Anon.)

---

## The upgrading document: developing a plan of action

The plan of action should include a research design and a research methodology suitable for the next stage of the work and achievable in the time available.

# 15 COMING TO TERMS WITH ORIGINALITY IN RESEARCH

*All good things which exist are the fruits of originality.*
(John Stuart Mill, *On Liberty* (1859), Ch. 1)

## The importance of originality in a research degree

For the purpose of upgrading a student's research degree to doctoral level, institutions require the proposed next stage of the work to show 'originality'. Although it could be argued that all research degrees should show originality to some extent, the originality required at doctoral level does normally need to be markedly and recognizably superior. Unless you are fortunate enough to have originality already built into your work in some way, developing it yourself is a threefold process. You need to appreciate the fullness and richness of what originality can mean – how it might be interpreted and how it might manifest itself. You need to learn and use creative skills to develop it. You also need to allow a considerable incubation period for these skills to function effectively. This chapter addresses the first of these, and Chapter 16 considers the use and incubation of creative skills. It is because of the incubation period that Chapter 1 warned at the outset that this chapter and the next should be studied fairly early on, even though making a case for originality would seldom be required until some time into a research programme.

A good way of coming to understand the fullness and richness of what originality can mean is through an analogy with an expedition of discovery. The research student is the explorer and the expedition is the research programme. For ease of writing, the explorer will be designated as male, although of course the research student could be of either sex. The explorer starts with a general idea of an area of land that he wishes to explore, just as the research student starts with a general area of interest.

## Originality in tools, techniques and procedures

In planning the expedition, the explorer uses what information he can to firm up on why he wants to explore the area and how he might do it, within the resources at his command and within any constraints that may exist. He uses his information to work out and organize what background knowledge, procedures, tools, equipment and personnel he will need, tailored to the resources and constraints. Some procedures may have to be specially designed, some tools and equipment may have to be specially made and some personnel may have to be specially trained or brought in.

Similarly, the research student studies the literature, talks to experts and sits in on relevant seminars or masters courses to get background knowledge and to develop an appropriate research methodology. This must include decisions about procedures, tools and techniques and possibly also people to be involved. Procedures, tools and techniques may be fairly standard in the field of study, but the research student may need to use them in new and untested ways or develop and make new ones for a specific purpose. The selection, development and testing of such procedures, tools and techniques could be the basis of the much sought-after originality.

## Originality in exploring the unknown

The expedition begins along the preplanned route. If this is previously unexplored, the mere exploration is original work. Similarly, if the research student is conducting a major investigation of something which has never been investigated before, such as a recently discovered insect, star or poem, the work will necessarily be original.

## Originality in exploring the unanticipated

The explorer's planned route may already have been broadly explored. However, he will, from time to time, come across unexpected and unexplored sidetracks. He may not notice them; or he may continue on the planned route anyway, in which case nothing original is involved.

If the explorer does notice the sidetracks, he has to make deci-sions about whether to explore any of them, and if so, which ones. These decisions may be difficult, because he cannot know whether anything of interest lies along them without at least partially explor-ing them, and doing so will use resources of time and equipment which may delay the expedition on its main route. Yet, one or more of these sidetracks could contain something of such great interest and importance that it would be worth abandoning the expedition as first planned and putting all the resources into exploring the sidetrack. Similarly, in fairly mundane research, one stage of the work can open up alternative ways forward which have never pre-viously been researched, and it is often these that can provide 'origi-nality', as well as the fascination with the unknown that ought to accompany research.

## Originality in use of data

The explorer may bring data back from the expedition which could not be processed on the expedition. Similarly, the research student may find himself or herself with much unprocessed data which he or she hopes may provide something 'original' when processed or analysed – perhaps a new theory or a verification or extension of an existing one. This is a perfectly possible way of incorporating origi-nality into work, but research students doing it need either good hunches about how the data might be used to advantage or consid-erable confidence in their creative abilities.

## Originality in outcomes

The explorer may bring back from the expedition all manner of goodies, from what he hoped for when he planned the expedition to the entirely unexpected. Similarly, the research student may de-velop outcomes which may or may not relate closely to the research problem as it was first formulated.

What the explorer may bring back could range from treasure with an obvious uniqueness, beauty and value, to items which were com-monplace where he explored, but unknown back home – like the potato which Sir Walter Raleigh brought to England from America. Similarly, original outcomes of research need not be new in absolute terms; they can simply be new to the situation, like tools, tech-niques and theories from one field of study, applied and evaluated in another.

## Originality in byproducts

Things may go so badly wrong on the explorer's expedition that it has to be abandoned with seemingly nothing achieved. Yet, with a little thought, he could still have an important story to tell. The illnesses of his team could, for example, be used to testify to the diseases that are rampant in the area. Or the torrential storms that washed away the collections of specimens could be monitored for interpretation in terms of what is already known about storms in that type of terrain. Neither of these would have been the purpose of the expedition, but they would be none the less valuable and provide 'originality'.

Similarly, the research student may be able to capitalize on everything that seems to go wrong. Important equipment may not work; crucial resources may not be available; people may not agree to be interviewed; funding may be withdrawn; or there may be other serious and unforeseen obstacles. Just as in the analogy, a little creative thinking can rescue the situation. There are almost always byproducts during any research, perhaps the development of a certain piece of equipment or some interesting secondary findings in the literature. These can be moved into the mainstream of the research, and focused on or developed further. When the thesis is written, the research problem merely needs to be reformulated to reflect the new nature of the work.

## Other interpretations and configurations of originality

There is really no limit to the variety of ways in which it is possible for research students to demonstrate originality in their work, and the above ideas and examples are intended merely to stimulate thought. The following activity aims to stimulate still more thought through the application of the above ideas to what could be possible in your own general field.

(■)  **Activity**

___

The following list was given in Box 5.6 of Chapter 5 as a checklist of possible solutions to research problems or other outcomes of research. Now, for your own general field, think of something for each item. It could be something that was original when it was first developed or something that would be original if it were developed in the future. It could even be something that you might develop yourself out of your own work. The emphasis is not on 'right answers' but on realizing that there really are a host of possibilities for originality in research, in all discipline areas, including your own.

- A new product


- A development of or an improvement on something which already exists


- A new theory


- A reinterpretation of an existing theory


- A new research tool or technique


- A new model or perspective


- An in-depth study


- A critical analysis


- A portfolio of work based on research


- A collection of generalizable findings or conclusions

⬛ **Discussion of activity**

Some examples are provided in Box 5.6 in Chapter 5, although yours, being in your own subject area, should be much more specialized. ⬛

## Recognizing originality with hindsight

Where the originality emerges as research progresses, it may be dramatically and immediately obvious. All too easily, however, it can be overlooked. To overcome this, it is worth regularly comparing the full scope of the work with other similar work in the field. Then something which was previously considered fairly mundane can reveal itself as having highly original potential which is worth developing further.

## The unpredictability of originality

Although 'originality' in some types of research is built in, in most fields of study it cannot be predicted in advance (see Box 15.1). Consequently, research students have to learn to live with a certain amount of uncertainty. This may be difficult, but it is a fact of research life, and can be ameliorated to some extent by welcoming the uncertainty as a precursor of creativity; thinking of the uncer-

---

**Box 15.1** Originality is unpredictable

A view from a Nobel laureate:

*In real life . . . the truth is not in nature waiting to declare itself and we cannot know a priori which observations are relevant and which are not; every discovery, every enlargement of the understanding begins as an imaginative preconception of what the truth might be. This imaginative preconception – a hypothesis – arises by a process as easy or as difficult to understand as any other creative act of mind; it is a brainwave, an inspired guess, the product of a blaze of light. It comes, anyway, from within and cannot be arrived at by the exercise of any known calculus of discovery.*

(Medawar, 1981, p. 84)

tainty as fascination with the unknown; and realizing that committed research students do normally manage to complete.

## Ownership of originality

When a team is working on a project, there is inevitable interaction between team members, and it may be difficult and even inappropriate to ascribe a particularly original insight or development to an individual. Research students working on such joint projects need to keep the negotiation of the boundaries of their contributions under regular review, because these will need to be documented in the thesis.

## Originality and the safety of the research degree

Since all research degrees are expected to show a certain amount of originality, the question is how much. On the face of it, the more stunning and original a new development is – the more it is a significant contribution to knowledge, a seminal work in the field, or a beneficial technological achievement – then the more highly it ought to be acclaimed. Unfortunately things do not always work like this, because it is a tendency of human nature for people to be slow to appreciate what is outside their understanding. Box 15.2 gives some examples.

Really original work is all too often slow to be accepted. To understand why, imagine overworked examiners faced with a thesis that is so original and significant that, if borne out, it would shake the very foundations of the subject. The first reaction of the examiners would be to wonder whether such a thesis really is valid. If it were, they might argue with themselves, then it would surely have come out of one of the major research centres, not from a mere research student. The examiners would realize that they would have to work through this thesis very carefully indeed, weighing every step of the argument and considering the reasonableness or otherwise of every piece of data, in order not to miss something that might invalidate the whole work. Even then, the examiners would fear that they still might overlook that crucial something. They know that if they ratify the thesis, its contents would spread like wildfire through the academic community; then someone else might find that something that actually invalidates everything. Then they, the examiners, would be seriously discredited.

So examiners' own reputations are at stake when they ratify a thesis. Consequently, before spending too much time on the details

---

**Box 15.2** The highly original may be the unappreciated

These are examples of three different kinds of innovative work which are now highly acclaimed and respected but were not accepted or appreciated at the time, almost certainly because others could not grasp what was outside their present understanding.

**Example 1:** Charlotte Brontë, who in the nineteenth century wrote the novel *Jane Eyre*, submitted some of her work to Robert Southey. At the time she was the unknown daughter of a Yorkshire parson and he was the poet laureate. He counselled her that her vivid imagination could give her brainfever and 'a distempered state of mind' and that 'literature cannot be the business of a woman's life'; he described her work to his friends as 'flighty'. Yet her work was soon to become much more famous and widely read than his. *The Guardian* (15 July 1995, p. 8) described the episode as 'one of the most notorious put-downs in the history of English literature'.

**Example 2:** Nowadays few people would deny the significance of the cheap production of the hormone progesterone, a constituent of the contraceptive pill. Yet when Russell Marker of Pennsylvania State College tried to interest drug companies in a cheap way to produce it in quantity, they were not interested. He could have given up, but instead he rented a small laboratory in Mexico City and began producing by himself. Several years later he arrived at a drug company with two jars, about 2 kg, of progesterone, equal to most of the world's supply at the time. When the company had recovered from the shock, they invited him to join them.

**Example 3:** The painter Van Gogh is reputed to have been so frustrated at his work, that he cut off his own ear in a fit of frenzy! Although there are various versions of this story, the fact remains that his works were not recognized in his lifetime and only remain today because his brother collected them. Now they hang in prestigious galleries all over the world.

---

of a highly original and significant thesis, there would be the temptation to check first on more mundane matters and put the problem off. This might result in their returning the thesis for clarification on a few issues or for rewriting of certain parts more in the language of

---

**Box 15.3**   Highly original articles and reactions of journal referees

*There is much evidence that the best papers are more likely to be rejected [when submitted for publication in journals]. 'Current Contents' ran some articles by the authors of the most cited papers in the physical and biological sciences – those that were cited more than 1000 times in ten years. The authors complained: 'I had more difficulty in getting this published than anything else I have written.' Some of the more prolific authors in economics and statistics have found the same: it is easy to place a routine paper but it is difficult to place an original, important or controversial paper. I know a case where one journal rejected a paper as rubbish, but another, of higher status, accepted it as being 'the most important paper ever published in this journal'.*

(Bowrick, 1995, p. 11)

---

academic discourse. Where examiners are faced with a highly original and significant thesis that relies on bringing different academic disciplines together, one of which is not their own, and which they do not really understand, their immediate reactions would be the same. The extract in Box 15.3 documents similar experiences of original and significant journal articles

Although not all examiners would behave in this way, it has to be said that research students with highly original and significant PhD theses do seem to have them referred (returned for alterations) much more often than research students with less original and significant ones. Many such students never bother to complete after a referral, and become totally disillusioned with academia.

The lesson is that research students whose work seems to be showing extreme originality and significance must be guided by their supervisors. The supervisor may warn against pursuing a highly original or significant theme, not because it is bad, but because it is unsafe. The supervisor may feel with some justification that the research student ought to be more established in the field before risking taking a novel idea further. On the other hand, the supervisor may see the original and significant work as lying entirely within his or her own competence and expertise. If such a supervisor belongs to an internationally renowned research group and publicly endorses the work, then it is well worth pursuing. The supervisor's backing should enable the thesis to be safe.

One of the safest and most common outcomes of a research degree is a set of findings or conclusions which are well substantiated through investigation and argument and which are generalizable from one situation to another. An example might be 'factors which facilitate crime on housing estates'. These might not set the academic world afire with their significance, but they could certainly claim to be original if the work had never been done before. Properly substantiated, the PhD would be safe because examiners would immediately recognize the value of the work.

## The status of originality in a research degree

Although originality is highly valued in research, it is not by itself enough. If it were, inventors would automatically earn higher degrees. Research competence is essential, i.e. the norms and codes of practice which ensure that a piece of research has the academic rigour to be convincing, backed by cogent argument and counter-argument.

Box 15.4 gives an extract on examples of originality generally, and Box 15.5 gives an extract on examples in hydraulics.

---

**Box 15.4**   General examples of originality

These examples of originality were collected from supervisors, examiners and research students by Estelle Phillips:

- *Carrying out empirical work that hasn't been done before.*
- *Making a synthesis that hasn't been made before.*
- *Using already known material but with a new interpretation.*
- *Trying out something in [one] country that has previously only been done in other countries.*
- *Taking a particular technique and applying it to a new area.*
- *Bringing new evidence to bear on an old issue.*
- *Being cross-disciplinary and using different methodologies.*
- *Looking at areas that people in the discipline haven't looked at before.*
- *Adding to knowledge in a way that hasn't been done before.*
                              (Zuber-Skerritt and Ryan, 1994, p. 139)

---

**Box 15.5**   Further examples of originality

These examples of originality were identified by a professor of hydraulics.

- *Setting down a major piece of new information in writing for the first time.*
- *Continuing a previously original piece of work.*
- *Carrying out original work designed by the supervisor.*
- *Providing a single original technique, observation or result in an otherwise unoriginal but competent piece of research.*
- *Having many original ideas, methods and interpretations, all performed by others under the direction of the postgraduate.*
- *Showing originality in testing somebody else's idea.*

(Francis, 1976)

# 16  DEVELOPING SKILLS FOR CREATIVE THINKING

*I envisage a dialogue between two voices, the one imaginative and the other critical.*

(Medawar, 1981, p. 85)

## The importance of creative thinking

Originality in some form is a crucial component of research at PhD level. Reasoned thinking alone is seldom enough (see Box 16.1). The development of original ideas can be enhanced through the use of various techniques to aid creative thinking. These are the subject of this chapter.

---

**Box 16.1**  Logical analysis and creativity

*If we look carefully at how creative, eminent scientists describe their own work, we find [a world] which uses logical analysis as a critical tool in the refinement of ideas, but which often begins in a very different place, where imagery, metaphor and analogy, intuitive hunches, kinesthetic feeling states, and even dreams or dream-like states are prepotent.*

(Bargar and Duncan, 1982, p. 3)

---

## Recognizing how intellectual creativity works

Creative thinking works differently for different people, so you need to recognize how it works for you. Try the following activity.

(■)   **Activity**

---

Think back to a number of difficult problems that you had to solve – ones that needed creative, i.e. novel or unusual, solutions, not just the application of some standard procedure or formula. The examples need not have to do with research or even with your subject. In fact, for this purpose, it is probably better if they are personal, family or financial. In each case write down some characteristics of the process by which you eventually arrived at the solutions. (What the solutions actually were is irrelevant.)

Now see if there is anything in common in the ways in which you developed solutions to these problems.

---

(■)   **Discussion of activity**

Most people find that some or all of the following are usually involved in arriving at a creative solution:

- There is a considerable mulling-over time before arriving at a solution, and there is no way of predicting how long this might be.
- The idea for a solution just pops into the mind, usually when not consciously thinking about it and when not thinking particularly hard about anything else either.
- Once the creative part of the problem-solving is over, hard groundwork still needs to be done to make a solution viable.

People who are familiar with techniques for creative thinking, invariably also include:

- The use of certain techniques can stimulate creative thinking.

Your list may even have included a creative thinking technique without your realizing that this was what it was – for example, talking things over with other people.  ●

## Techniques to facilitate creative thinking

Some techniques which facilitate creative thinking are well known and well practised because they are common sense, second nature or fundamental to good research. Others are not widely known, which is a pity because research students who do know about them usually find them very useful. The next few sections present a selection. For others, see the Further Reading section. You will probably find that some creative thinking techniques suit you and some do not, but it is a good idea to bear a number in mind, and try them from time to time. You only need one really good idea to set your research off in a viable direction.

## Talking things over

Talking things over with other people not only provides the benefit of their views and ideas. The very act of talking seems to stimulate one's own thinking. Whether or not the other person needs to be an expert in the field must depend on the nature of the problem. Although one would, for example, go to an expert for expert information, that is not at all the same as facilitating one's own creativity. This merely requires someone of sound judgement who can supply time and commitment. You might choose other research students or members of your family, particularly if they happen to have an academic background.

## Keeping an open mind

Keeping an open mind should be fundamental to all research, but it can also be used as a technique for creative thinking. It involves identifying all the unlikely or seemingly implausible interpretations and then considering them carefully to see if they might have any validity. Keeping an open mind is particularly important when talking to others; without it, you are liable to hear only what you already know.

## Brainstorming

Brainstorming is a well-known problem-solving technique, particularly in groups. It is mentioned here for comprehensiveness, although it seems to be the least useful technique for the sorts of problem and issue that research students have to address. It consists of listing as many ways forward as possible, however improbable, without pausing to evaluate them. Only when the list is complete may the value and feasibility of the possibilities be considered.

## Negative brainstorming

Negative brainstorming is a technique that can be of considerable use for the sorts of problems and issues that research students have to address, and is suitable for individual as well as group use. It consists of listing as many ways as one can think of about how not to achieve a purpose, and then, when the list is complete, considering whether reversing any of them might be productive.

The idea of negative brainstorming may seem rather trite, and most of the reversed ideas often turn out to be meaningless. Nevertheless, it can produce ideas that would never have been thought of using more direct methods, and only one needs to be worthwhile.

## Viewing the problem from imaginative perspectives

This is a technique that frees the mind from constraints which may have handicapped its creative thinking and which may in practice not be as binding as convention and normal expectations have led one to expect. The technique consists of giving the imagination free rein on the problem or issue in ways that may seem preposterous, to see if they generate any ideas that could be turned into something worthwhile. One asks oneself how one would feel about the problem or issue if one was, say, in outer space, or 200 years into the future, or living the sort of lifestyle that one has always dreamed of.

This is a very valuable technique for research students (see, for example, the anecdote in Box 16.2).

---

**Box 16.2**   Creativity and imaginative perspectives

Einstein is reputed to have begun working on his theory of relativity by giving his imagination free rein and wondering what it would be like to ride on a light ray.

---

## Concentrating on anomalies

The technique of concentrating on anomalies can also be extremely important and useful for research students. Many researchers tend to concentrate on what they believe to be the main theme or central issue of their research, and when they come across some aspect that does not fit, they ignore it. The technique of concentrating on anomalies involves focusing on these anomalies and making a feature of them to see if they offer anything worth exploring or investigating. The anecdote in Box 16.3 is an example.

---

**Box 16.3** Creativity and focusing on anomalies

The anecdote in Box 5.4 in Chapter 5 is also an example of the value of focusing on anomalies. When Joscelyn Bell Burnell, then an astronomy research student at Cambridge, noticed unexpected scuffs on her photographic plates while she was routinely surveying the night sky, she could have ignored them or assumed they were dirt. However, she chose to investigate the scuffs, which resulted in the major discovery of 'pulsars'.

---

## Focusing on byproducts

Focusing on byproducts is another technique which is particularly useful for research students who can be so committed to the main theme of their research that they do not recognize the significance of something that may have happened or that they may have developed along the way. Box 16.4 gives an example.

---

**Box 16.4** Creativity and byproducts

It is said that the antibiotic penicillin would never have been discovered if Sir Alexander Fleming had not been interested enough to bother to investigate a stray contamination of mould.

---

## Interrogating imaginary experts

The technique of interrogating imaginary experts consists of imagining that you are able to interview and interrogate a real or imaginary expert in your field, and preparing some suitable questions. These often turn out to be surprisingly perceptive; and they may open up some unexpectedly original and valuable ways forward for your research.

## Viewing the problem from the perspective of another discipline

Pushing back the frontiers of knowledge in a single discipline can be a rather formidable way of producing original and significant work. Often a simpler alternative is to see what can be achieved by bringing different disciplines together. A technique is to talk the problem or issue over with people from other disciplines to see how they would approach it. Or, if you happen to have a sound grounding in another discipline yourself, perhaps from your undergraduate work, or if you would feel stimulated to learn more about that discipline, you could try viewing the problem yourself from the perspective of that discipline. You may not need to have any great expertise in it. The anecdotes in Box 16.5 give examples.

---

**Box 16.5**   Creativity and linking with other disciplines

**Example 1:** Sir Alexander Graham Bell had a deaf wife and therefore was interested in developing a device that would amplify sound. He was a biologist by training, and he applied what he knew about the form of the human ear to develop the telephone. It is said that if he had just been a physicist, the idea of developing a telephone would have appeared too daunting ever to attempt.

**Example 2:** Crick and Watson were not molecular biologists. If they had been they might not have dared to propose their model for DNA.

---

## Using 'the solution looking for the problem': serendipity

A good creative technique is to keep one's eyes and ears constantly open, to question anything and everything to see if it might be used to provide a creative leap forward. The anecdotes in Box 16.6 are examples.

---

**Box 16.6**  Creativity and serendipity

**Example 1:** It is unlikely that anyone looking for a way of speeding customers through supermarket checkouts would have thought of developing the laser as a means of solving the problem. The fact was that the laser was there, already developed, and someone was bright enough to spot a new use for it. Other bright people have of course spotted other practical uses for it in a wide variety of different areas – replacing torn eye retinas, for example.

**Example 2:** George de Mestral had no intention of inventing the Velcro fastener when he looked to see why burs stuck tightly to his clothing.

---

## Using mind maps

A mind map is a technique for freeing the mind from the single, constrained and traditional viewpoint from which it has been seeing a problem or issue. It provides an overview, which shows at a glance all the components of the problem or issue and the links between them. This tends to stimulate new and creative ideas. The technique is best explained by working through the next activity. Much has been written on mind maps (see the Further Reading section).

⬛  **Activity**

---

To illustrate the procedure for making a mind map, think of a problem or issue which is currently concerning you. In order to illustrate the method, it may be best to make this fairly trivial, like what to have for supper or where to go next weekend, although if you prefer a research problem, feel free to choose one.

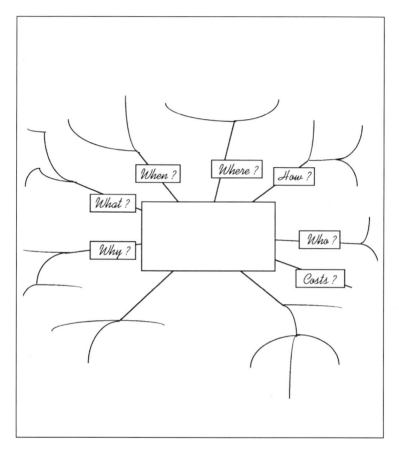

*Figure 16.1*

On the diagram in Figure 16.1:

- Write down what the problem or issue is inside the blank box.
- Note the seven spokes coming out of the box, labelled: why? what? when? where? who? how? and costs?
- Label the remaining two spokes coming out of the title box with other questions that seem appropriate to the problem or issue, and draw more spokes and label them if you think there are further appropriate questions.

- Let your mind wander over the questions on each spoke and label keywords for your thoughts, any thoughts, on the further spokes.
- Draw more spokes, as the labelled ideas suggest further ideas, and label these new spokes, which may link up with existing ones.

Continue until you run out of ideas. Then note any similar labels which are common to more than one spoke.

You may feel that a viable solution has already occurred to you. If not, put the paper aside and see if a solution pops into your head later.

---

(■)    **Discussion of activity**

Mind maps have widespread applicability in a variety of tasks that require creative thinking. They can, for example, with suitably labelled spokes, also be used to generate the content of reports, thesis chapters and presentations. Possible spoke labels might be 'purpose of report, chapter or presentation', 'links with previous knowledge', 'work to be reported', 'constraints on work' and 'outcomes'. Once the mind map has produced the ideas for content, these still have to be structured into a meaningful order, but that is a separate activity.                                                                   (■)

### Creativity and free time

Solutions only pop into one's mind if it is not occupied, i.e. it is thinking about nothing in particular. The anecdotes in Box 16.7 are

---

**Box 16.7**   Creativity and letting the mind wander freely

**Example 1:** The mathematician Poincaré claimed to have thought of his most profound idea quite suddenly while boarding a bus.

**Example 2:** In the middle of the nineteenth century the constituent atoms of a molecule of benzene were known, but no stable molecular structure could be visualized. The problem was solved by Kekulé, who, while musing in a semi-dozing state, visualized snakes coiling round eating their own tails. This gave him the idea, which has since come to be accepted, that the benzene molecule could be in the form of a ring.

examples. So, although it is important for research students to study hard, doing it all the time is counter-productive. Take a few minutes over the following activity, to think about how to help your creative abilities operate.

 **Activity**

List activities which you enjoy and are practical for you to indulge in, and which free your mind from purposeful thinking.

 **Discussion of activity**

You have probably identified some form of sport, or something like gardening, listening to music, or yoga. Perhaps you should force yourself to spend more time on these mind-freeing activities. Television and reading may be relaxing but they are unlikely to be appropriate for freeing the mind for creativity.

Many people find that creative ideas just pop into their mind when they wake up in the night, still half asleep. They recommend keeping a pen and paper beside the bed for jotting the ideas down, for full consideration later.                                              ■

 **Activity**

Assume that you want to develop your research in a new direction. Try each of the following creative techniques:

• Negative brainstorming
• Viewing the problem from imaginative perspectives
• Concentrating on anomalies

- Focusing on byproducts
- Interrogating imaginary experts
- Viewing the problem from the perspective of another discipline.

Do not expect any dramatic ideas to emerge until some time in the future, when your mind has had time to mull things over.

---

### Creativity and routine work

Having a good idea is not enough on its own to merit a research degree. You must work on it, to turn it into an approach, tool, model, theory, etc. that is convincingly tested and is justified according to the academic rigour of the subject. Such work is likely to be fairly routine, but it is none the less crucial. Failure to apply it will lead to a failed thesis.

### Creativity and planning

Much of research is routine and straightforward, and is most efficiently carried out by careful planning. However, all good research must also involve a certain amount of creativity which cannot be done to command or deadlines. This can and will sabotage plans about where research students would like their work to be by a particular time. Be aware of this, and realize when it happens that it is normal.

# 17 DEALING WITH FLAGGING

*Ultimately, there are aspects of [research] students' adaptation to their new role which appear to be partially dependent on their particular character.*

(Hockey, 1994, p. 188)

## Understanding and coping with flagging

A research degree involves a commitment over several years. It means working independently, often in isolation; and it involves coping with the unexpected and with things going wrong. In addition, there may be family matters, career matters and financial matters which keep emerging to detract from concentration on the research. It is hardly a wonder that research students go through periods of doubting the value of what they are doing and whether it is worth continuing.

Self-doubt and flagging are quite normal, and you need to understand that this is so. Nevertheless, their effects can be minimized in three ways. The first is by talking things through with others – and you were alerted in Chapter 4 to put effort into finding suitable people as early as possible in your research programme. The second is by maintaining a balanced outlook through a healthy lifestyle of sensible eating and appropriate exercise; and the third is to find out about common causes and how best to deal with them. It is with the latter that this chapter should help.

## Lacking a sense of direction

Feeling that you do not know where you are going with your research can have a variety of causes.

Research students often feel that their lack of direction is due to lack of support or expert knowledge from their supervisors, although this is not at all necessarily the case. A supervisor's task is not to

---

**Box 17.1**  Don't quit!

*When things go wrong as they sometimes will,*
*When the road you're trudging seems all up hill,*
*When funds are low and the debts are high,*
*And you want to smile, but you have to sigh,*
*When care is pressing you down a bit,*
*Rest, if you must – but don't you quit.*

*Life is queer with its twists and turns*
*As everyone of us sometimes learns*
*And many a failure turns about*
*When he might have won had he stuck it out;*
*Don't give up, though the pace seems slow –*
*You might succeed with another blow.*

*Often the goal is nearer than*
*it seems to a faint and faltering man,*
*Often the struggler has given up*
*When he might have captured the victor's cup.*
*And he learned too late, when the night slipped down,*
*How close he was to the golden crown.*

*Success is failure turned inside out –*
*The silver tint of the clouds of doubt –*
*And you never can tell how close you are,*
*It may be near when it seems afar;*
*So, stick to the fight when you're hardest hit –*
*It's when things seem worst that you mustn't quit.*

(Anon.)

---

lead every step of the way; research students are expected to act independently, following their own ideas – under, of course, the watchful eyes of supervisors to advise and warn. If you think that this may be your problem, the answer is to start taking responsibility for yourself. If, after sufficient thought, you really do think that another supervisor would help, be resolute, and set about making it happen. Chapter 6 outlines possible procedures.

A common reason for lacking a sense of direction is that research students know that originality needs to be built into their work, particularly for a PhD, but are uncertain how. This is a particular problem for students working in isolation on topics which are of no particular interest to anyone nearby. If this is what you perceive as your problem, its recognition is itself the first step to the solution. The explorer analogy in Chapter 15 should set you thinking. Ideas which are specific for your own research require creative thought. So try some of the techniques of Chapter 16. If your lack of direction is because you are waiting for a creative idea to strike, you have no option but to allow yourself a short period of not worrying about it while you wait; so take a break. If that period seems set to become unacceptably long, keep reusing the techniques of Chapter 16. Giving up on identifying or developing originality is not an option unless you are prepared to give up being a doctoral student.

## Aiming for perfection

Research students ought to be vigilant to ensure that their work is good enough for the research degree for which they are registered. It is not necessary to aim for perfection which is unattainable anyway.

Research needs to be convincing by conforming to the normal research practices of the discipline. If you need to be reminded of what these are, Chapter 5 should help. A more detailed understanding needs to be developed over time through reading the literature in your subject, discussing with your supervisor and attending departmental seminars or training sessions for research students. Your aims should be to reach a stage where you feel confident monitoring your own standards.

Research at doctoral level needs to be original, independent and significant. Chapter 15 considers the various manifestations and configurations of originality, and Chapter 16 presents techniques to help develop it. Independence could be a problem where a team project is concerned, but with care and attention to the boundaries of individual contributions, and goodwill and professionalism all round, it seldom is. There is a view that all new knowledge must be significant, but the nature of acceptable significance does depend on the norms of the discipline. Discussion and reading are the ways to discover the norms in your discipline.

It is natural at times for research students to feel that their work is rather trivial and to strive for a perfectionism that is not only time-consuming but also unobtainable. Be guided by your supervisor on this. If you would appreciate the reassurance of other people who are experienced in what makes a research degree, give a departmental seminar where other research students and academic staff can give their opinions on your work.

## Worrying about being pipped at the post

Research students can feel like giving up when they learn that some-one, somewhere is working on the same problem and is likely to finish sooner. This is something that they must discuss with their super-visors, because supervisors know the work, the general field and the regulations of the institution. You must let your supervisor guide you.

In practice, the matter may not be particularly serious. Even if the other work is identical, which is most likely to occur in science-based subjects, it normally takes some months for research findings to reach the stage of journal publication, and most institutional regulations will allow a breathing space for a thesis to go forward provided that this is sufficiently short to guarantee that the work is the research student's own.

In the humanities and social sciences, the chances are that the work is only broadly similar. Then the thing to do is to contact the other researchers to find out precisely what they have done. It is bound to be different in some way: perhaps in the research design, or the sample, or the precision of the result. You would merely need to build a new section into your thesis to compare and contrast the work with your own, drawing some meaningful conclusions.

## Feeling disorganized

The independence which research students have can mean that it is all too easy to waste time talking to people, drinking coffee and pop-ping out to the shops. Research students need to plan their work and manage themselves and their time. If this is your problem, Chapters 8, 9 and 10 should be helpful. Nevertheless, knowing what to do is not the same as doing it. So you will have to learn self-discipline.

Your problem may be that you are working so hard that you cannot think straight. Then you must take a break or even a short holiday, so as to refresh yourself. Not only is there nothing at all wrong in doing this, it is probably essential if you are to continue the programme effectively and efficiently.

## Losing interest, becoming bored and getting depressed

Research should be intellectually fascinating because it involves discovering or developing something new in an area that should have considerable personal appeal. Nevertheless, it is natural to lose interest or become bored at times. It is often helpful to have several themes on the go at once, so that there is more likely to be something tempting to work on.

You may be at a stage where your work genuinely is excessively routine and monotonous. Some people find that it helps to listen to light music during tasks which do not require much concentration. Monotonous stages in research should pass. If they look unlikely to do so, a solution could be to take up an alternative direction or approach (see the explorer analogy of Chapter 15).

Some reasons for getting depressed are intensely personal. It is difficult to concentrate on doing good research if you have personal, financial, career or health problems. This is where the support of others is so important, as they can often recognize and diagnose the cause of the problem before you can yourself. Listen to them and allow them to support you. Also, if it seems appropriate, make use of institutional counselling services. Most are excellent as well as confidential. There are few personal problems that professional counsellors have not seen before and they can often point to sources of help.

For short-term depression, many people find that certain pieces of music can be mood-enhancing. For longer-term or more serious depression, do not make quick decisions about giving up. Find and use the support you need. Then you may feel differently before too long. If, after a time, you still feel like giving up, take a holiday. If, even then, you still feel like giving up, this may of course be the right decision for you. Before you do give up, though, talk with your supervisor. This may be difficult because you may feel that you are letting him or her down, but there is little that upsets a good supervisor more than a student just disappearing.

## Interacting ineffectually with associates

It is self-evident that research students need to be able to interact effectively with other people. Chapters 6 and 11 respectively consider the specifics of interacting as a research student with a supervisor and more generally with other people. The problem of interacting as an individual is too wide-ranging to be considered here. It requires the help and support of someone who either cares about you or is a professional counsellor.

## Getting nowhere

Research students normally feel better about seeming to get nowhere if they realize that, minor problems and mishaps apart, it is a fundamental feature of research that it seldom goes according to plan (see Box 17.2). No one is responsible, although it is the research student who has to find a way of compensating.

Also research invariably goes more slowly than anticipated. So the feeling of getting nowhere is to be expected, provided that it doesn't last too long. It isn't that a jinx is on an individual or an indication that the individual isn't up to the job. Small problems can normally be sorted out quite easily by keeping on good terms with others in the department: other students, academics, secretaries, technicians, etc. Then supervisors do not have to be disturbed unnecessarily.

It is often the case that research students think they are getting nowhere because they are so close to what they are doing that they do not spot where a slight change of direction or emphasis could lead to something much more meaningful. That is why taking time off is so important, as of course is appreciating the various forms in which quality work can manifest itself or be developed (see Chapters 15 and 16).

---

**Box 17.2** The rational model of how research should operate doesn't work

*[ The rational model for the conduct of research] is perhaps an idealised guide to how research ought to be conducted. [It] does not attempt to provide an accurate description of the process whereby research actually is conducted. At the present time, to my knowledge, a commonly accepted descriptive model of the research process is not available.*

(Martin, 1982, p. 19)

---

## Frustrated at the difficulties of part-time study

For research students in full-time employment, it is particularly difficult having to do research work in the evenings and at weekends. Not only are they tired and missing out on social activities with family and friends, but also various resources, such as specialist libraries or laboratories, may not be open at accessible times. If you get frustrated about this, it is understandable. If you can argue that your research supports your paid work in some way, it may be possible to negotiate some measure of flexitime with your job, or time off during the day. If not, you certainly need the emotional and practical support of the people close to you. Remember that committed people in your situation do successfully complete their research degrees – and in sizeable numbers.

## Facing a time-consuming emergency

If you are going through an emergency which needs a great deal of time and energy to handle, such as illness, you may find it helpful to take take time out, rather than to try to cope ineffectively with too many things at the same time. Most institutions have a category of registration for students who are forced to interrupt their studies, but who intend to continue at a later date. No fee is levied for this category and the time out does not count towards the required period of registration. Funding bodies may not be as sympathetic as institutions; so the position does need to be explored with them.

A common alternative is to switch from full-time to part-time study. There are also other categories of registration, and it is important for your finances as well as your time management that you are registered in the most appropriate category. Changes of registration category should, if possible, be discussed with supervisors well in advance of the term in which the change is to take place, and approval must then be given by the institution.

## Feeling stressed and unable to cope

Everyone goes through phases of feeling emotionally wound up or drained and unable to cope. Research students are no exception. If the reason is not one of those already mentioned, it is probably because they are overworked and need regular exercise, a break or a holiday. They may need to see a counsellor or doctor.

Box 17.3 gives some common and quite general reasons for feeling stressed. You may like to compare them with what you are experiencing.

## Wanting to get on with the next stage of life

It is understandable for research students to want to get on with the next stage of their lives. In particular, it is tempting to accept a good job offer if it comes up, assuming that the thesis can then be finished during odd evenings and weekends. In fact, this is an extremely difficult thing to do, and it is one of the most widespread reasons for

---

**Box 17.3** Causes of stress at work

Fontana (1993) lists *general* causes of stress under the following headings:

- *Organizational problems*
- *Insufficient backup*
- *Long or unsociable hours*
- *Poor status, pay and promotion prospects*
- *Unnecessary rituals and procedures*
- *Uncertainty and insecurity.*

As for *specific* causes of stress at work, Fontana lists the following:

- *Unclear role specifications*
- *Role conflict*
- *Unrealistically high expectations (perfectionism)*
- *Inability to influence decision-making (powerlessness)*
- *Frequent clashes with supervisors*
- *Isolation from colleagues' support*
- *Overwork and time pressures*
- *Lack of variety*
- *Poor communication*
- *Inadequate leadership*
- *Conflicts with colleagues*
- *Inability to finish a job*
- *Fighting unnecessary battles.*

---

not completing a PhD. So think carefully before taking any action in this respect that you may later regret.

## Not wanting to get on with the next stage of life

Being a research student does offer a form of security – belonging to a community, being cared for by a professional, etc. – and this can make some research students *not* want to get on with the next stage of their lives. The problem has to be recognized and faced up to. It cannot be allowed to go on for ever. The best solution is to talk it through with someone responsible and caring, perhaps the institutional counsellor.

(■)  **Activity**

If you feel yourself flagging, where, in view of the above sections, do you think the problem lies, and what can you do about it?

From your experience or from the advice of others, what pieces of music are most likely to help you:

• as background for routine work

• for improving your mood

Should you take more exercise or eat more healthily?

## Concluding remarks

There can be many reasons for a thesis being delayed or never even completed. The extract in Box 17.4 gives some reasons identified by the former Science and Engineering Research Council. The Further Reading section references a book on ten students' experiences of the PhD process; it is essential reading for all research students who think that their problems are unique, and who want some encouragement.

---

**Box 17.4**  Research council identifies reasons for delay and non-completion

*It is worth looking at some of the reasons for long completion times or failure to complete ... One quite common reason for late completion [is] a slow start ... If insufficient effort is put into the formulation of the problem, to making a literature survey where appropriate, or such other initial activities as are desirable, the result is that the remaining portion of ... activities is always a scramble and the programme inevitably slips.*

---

A second common cause of delay is the student who is never satisfied. He can always think of a way of improving his results. In short, he cannot bring anything to a conclusion. Perfectionism can be a virtue, but if only a student would write up what he had achieved, he would almost certainly see more clearly whether any improvement was actually necessary, the amount of effort required if it was desirable, or whether it was sensible to attempt that amount of work in the time available . . .

A third common cause of delay is distraction from the main line of enquiry. These days a common distraction is for a student to get 'hooked on' computing with the result that he over analyses his experimental data, largely because of the sheer pleasure he gets out of manipulating the computer; but with inevitable delays. leading to a delayed thesis . . .

When the work has gone well and opened up prospects for future research, the supervisor may in some subjects suggest that the student might like to consider a two or three year continuation as a post-doctoral research assistant. Experience shows that if the student accepts, and is appointed before handing in his thesis, in the vast majority of cases the progress on the thesis slows dramatically.

(Science and Engineering Research Council, 1992)

# 18 PRODUCING YOUR THESIS

*Many research students believe that the quality of a thesis necessarily improves with the amount of time taken to prepare it and the number of words it contains. This is not true.*

(Economic and Social Research Council, 1986, p. 13)

## The importance of the thesis

The thesis is the culmination of a research student's entire research programme, and it is on the thesis that he or she will be examined and judged. So it is in your best interests to make yours good. A thesis is much more than a report of work. This chapter gives some advice on producing it. The suggestions are general and will not be entirely appropriate for all fields of study, as there is no consistent view across disciplines about what constitutes an acceptable research degree thesis. Nevertheless, the chapter should stimulate your thinking and indicate topics for discussion and clarification.

## Orientating yourself for the task ahead

As an orientation for producing a thesis, it is useful to return to the analogy of the explorer. Knowing that he will be telling his story when he gets home, the explorer will keep careful and detailed records during the expedition. These are the equivalent of research students' logs, diaries, draft theses, etc. He may start writing his story, as a story, while still on the expedition – just as research students may find that it aids their thinking to write draft thesis chapters and have a thesis outline as they go along. However, he will know that how he eventually tells the story will, with hindsight, be different in sequence, scope and emphasis. So it is with a thesis.

There are a number of points that the explorer will bear in mind, when he comes to tell his story after the expedition. He will want to stress the novelty and value of the outcomes. Although he will include what he hoped at the outset that the general outcomes might be, he will give most attention to features of special importance that may or may not have been predicted in advance, such as finding hidden treasure, or special procedures developed for successfully tracking a certain animal, etc. So he will not necessarily tell the story in the order in which things happened, nor will he give every period of the expedition an equal slot of story time or length – although he may mention chronological development as a justification or explanation in connection with something else. Similarly, the final version of the thesis should be written, with hindsight, knowing where one has been. It should take the reader naturally and convincingly to the major outcomes, which may or may not have been anticipated at the outset. The introduction should be drafted early to orientate yourself for writing what is to follow. (However, as the thesis itself will go through a number of drafts, the introduction will need to be finalized much later in order to orientate the reader properly.)

The explorer will vary his way of telling his story according to the audience. The crucially important audience for theses are external examiners. Think of them as individuals who are exceptionally busy and grossly underpaid, and who therefore have to read theses quickly. They will expect them to be well structured and to be argued coherently to make the case for certain solutions to specific research problems. Irrelevances will irritate, as will having to tease out meaning that research students should have extracted themselves. Think of them also as individuals who are very able and experienced in the general area, which means that background material should be as concise as is consistent with showing that it is known.

However, no external examiner can be an expert in your work. By the time you finalize your thesis, you and you alone are the world's expert. So the aspects that make your work significant, original and worthy of a PhD or a MPhil, need to be argued cogently: each step needs to be spelt out; the outcomes must be stated unambiguously and all their implications identified and discussed in depth.

## Developing a framework of chapters

A thesis should have one or more storylines running through. A good way to develop the framework is to draft out the case on which the thesis is based, and then see what aspects seem to substantiate it or carry it forward such that they merit chapters in their own right. Likely components would be the following, some of which will require several chapters, depending on the nature of the work:

- the research area and how the research problem or topic was identified and refined;
- discussion leading to statements of the research methodology for the various themes of the research problem or topic;
- reports on work done, including the emerging data and its analysis;
- solutions to the research problem (outcomes) and a discussion of their applicability, limitations, and the scope for further work.

The emphasis placed on a literature survey chapter in its own right depends on the field of study. Where it is usual to define the research problem early on and to keep it relatively unchanged, a separate literature survey chapter is the norm, to set the scene for what lies ahead. In fields of study where it is usual for the direction of each stage of the research to rely on findings of an earlier stage, new literature may need to be incorporated at each stage. Many theses will require a balance, with relevant information from the literature running to a greater or lesser extent through all the components.

Also running through all the components of the thesis should be the identification of relevant background knowledge, as well as difficulties and constraints, and how they were handled.

(■)   **Activity**

---

In your field of study, how normal is it for almost all the literature survey material to be in a single chapter?

Is it normal or necessary for there to be more, fewer or different components than those listed above?

---

(■) **Discussion of activity**

Irrespective of whether a literature survey is considered worthy of a chapter in its own right, do continually bear in mind, as pointed out in Chapter 12, that literature should be used to substantiate and carry forward arguments and counter-arguments. It should not read as a catalogue of vaguely relevant material, even though it is wise to find a way of bringing in all the important works in the field.

Where it is normal for research students to have an outline of their thesis from an early stage, which they modify and add to as the work progresses, this can provide an excellent basis for the framework of chapters. (■)

## Developing the content of a chapter

When developing the material to go into any chapter, the following checklist may be a useful starting point to stimulate further thinking:

- The purposes of the chapter
- Links with other knowledge (e.g. earlier or later chapters or the work of other people)
- Constraints
- Work carried out
- Outcomes
- Where next?

It may be that much of the substance of chapters may be obtained by lifting sections directly out of earlier reports. The chances are, however, that they will need editing to reflect a more recently emerged coherence.

If you can work with mind maps (see Chapter 16), a useful technique is to use one for developing ideas for the content of a chapter. It enables your creativity to have full rein. The above bullet points can serve as spokes.

(■) **Activity**

Get a feel for using a mind map to develop content by producing one on a separate sheet of paper. Label the spokes with the bullet points above. If you are not ready to do a chapter, experience the technique by using it to develop the content of a report or essay.

The purpose is merely to set your mind thinking on this use of mind maps, not to develop any lasting content.

---

(■)  **Discussion of activity**

Developing material to go into a chapter is a separate activity from putting it into a logical order. This is considered in the next section.

(■)

## Sequencing the content of a chapter

There is no single right way of sequencing material within a chapter. This is a lesson worth learning because some research students waste considerable time searching for it. What matters is that the sequencing should be acceptable, irrespective of whether it could be done differently. There needs to be an internal logic. If the chapter contains more than one stream of argument, they need to be linked by careful structuring and cross-referencing. It may be worth referring to Chapter 12 on structuring a report, because much of it can be adapted for structuring a thesis chapter.

As you write, amendments to content and structure will suggest themselves – often as a result of the highly productive exercise of arguing with yourself as you write.

## Linking chapters to develop a storyline

Chapters of a thesis should link together to make a unified whole with one or more storylines. The technique of developing and demonstrating a storyline was introduced in Chapter 12, but for a thesis, being so much longer and having several themes, it is even more useful. So it is always worth wording the headings of chapters and sections so that they convey as comprehensively as possible what is in them. Then it is helpful to keep an up-to-date contents list, as you work, to be able to see the developing storyline at a glance. It is here that any lack of coherence is likely to show up first; so the technique can save hours of writing that would later have to be discarded.

It should be clear to a reader from the first paragraph of a chapter where the chapter fits into the rest of the thesis. The first step is to write a few keywords or some notes under each of the following headings:

- Setting the scene for the chapter, i.e. the general area(s) that the chapter considers.
- The gap in knowledge or understanding which the chapter addresses – usually as identified as an issue in (an) earlier chapter(s).
- How the chapter fills the gap.
- A brief overview of what is in the chapter.

Then edit the notes together to form the introduction to the chapter. Box 18.1 illustrates the technique.

---

**Box 18.1** A technique for developing the introductory paragraph of a thesis chapter

*Notes are written under each of the bullet points:*

- *Setting the scene for the chapter, i.e. the general area(s) that the chapter considers, e.g.:*

  The chapter is about self-instruction, universities, Sierra Leone.

- *The gap in knowledge or understanding which the chapter addresses – usually as identified as an issue in (an) earlier chapter(s), e.g.:*

  Self-instruction is not used in universities in Sierra Leone although Chapter 3 shows that it has proved useful in other countries.

- *How the chapter fills the gap, e.g.:*

  The chapter suggests ways in which self-instruction might be used for teaching English as a foreign language in the national university of Sierra Leone.

• *A brief overview of what is in the chapter, e.g.:*

The chapter surveys and draws conclusions from the very limited use of self-instruction over the last twenty years in other subject areas and at various educational levels in Sierra Leone.

*The notes are edited together to form the introductory paragraph, e.g.:*

Self-instruction for teaching undergraduates is little used in Sierra Leone, even though the evidence from Chapter 3 shows that it has proved useful in other countries. This chapter suggests ways in which self-instruction might be used as a means of teaching English as a foreign language in the national university of Sierra Leone. It does this on the basis of surveying and discussing the very limited use of self-instruction over the last twenty years in other subject areas and at various educational levels in Sierra Leone.

(Author's workshop handout)

The concluding paragraph of a chapter should show how its theme is carried on elsewhere in the thesis. The technique for doing this consists of writing a few keywords or some notes under each of the following headings:

• What the chapter has done
• What new questions the chapter has identified
• Where these questions are dealt with.

Then edit the notes together. Box 18.2 illustrates the technique.

**Box 18.2**   A technique for developing the concluding paragraph of a thesis chapter

*Notes are written under each of the bullet points:*

• *What the chapter has done, e.g.:*

Concluded that self-instruction could work well for teaching English as a foreign language in the national university of Sierra Leone.

- *What new questions the chapter has identified, e.g.:*

  How the self-instructional materials should be developed and produced and how the teachers should be trained to use them.

- *Where these questions are dealt with, e.g.:*

  The questions are dealt with in Chapters 7 and 8.

*The notes are edited together to form a concluding paragraph, e.g.:*

This chapter has concluded that self-instruction could be usefully employed to teach English as a foreign language in the national university of Sierra Leone. It has raised questions about how the self-instructional materials should be developed and produced, and how the teachers should be trained to use them. These questions are respectively addressed in Chapters 7 and 8.

(Author's workshop handout)

⬛ **Activity**

Assume that you are about to write the introduction to a chapter of your thesis. If you are not ready to do this yet, practise the technique on any other piece of writing, such as an essay or report. Write a few keywords or some notes under each of the above headings and then edit them together into an introduction.

Imagine that you are about to write the concluding paragraph to a chapter of your thesis. Write a few keywords or some notes under each of the above headings and then edit them together into a concluding paragraph.

## Cross-referencing in the thesis

A document as large as a thesis will inevitably require cross-references between sections and chapters, but during the drafting stage it is not possible to know the precise page of the cross-reference. A helpful tip is to call it page 00 or section 00, in line with the practice employed by various publishing houses. This signifies that a number is to be put in later. Then at the stage of the final printout, all that is necessary is to use the 'find' command of the word processor to locate all the 00s and replace them with a number which is now known. This is much easier than having to read through to locate all instances where a reference number is needed.

## The writing process

Writing a thesis is generally a matter of progressively refining chapters in the light of their internal consistency and their relationship to other chapters. This cannot be done quickly, and most research students underestimate the time needed for it.

It is not usually worth trying to write the chapters of a thesis in sequence. Start with a chapter or several chapters that are currently fascinating you or that you have already come to grips with in your mind. Then develop them in whatever way is easiest for you, be it text on a computer, or scribble on blank sheets of paper, or as a 'mind map'. The emphasis should be on producing a coherent structure, rather than on grammar or style. When you come to do the actual writing, it is probably best to do your own typing on a word processor so that you can make revisions easily as they occur to you. Then use the 'drawer treatment' as described in Chapter 12.

Ask your supervisor at what stage he or she would like to see the drafts. The usual procedure is for research students to write a chapter of a thesis, submit it to their supervisors and then rewrite to accommodate comments, but it is a mistake then to believe that the revised chapter is completely finished, never to need further modification. The 'storyline' of a thesis can never be clear from a single chapter. The full thesis is required, at least in draft. No supervisor will finally 'approve' a chapter in isolation. The scene-setting chapters are most likely to remain unchanged, but the analytical and interpretative ones depend too much on one another. Realize that, according to most institutional regulations, the decision that a thesis is ready to submit is the research student's, not the supervisor's. That is why 'approve' is in inverted commas, and it applies to the entire thesis as well as to any single chapter.

Updating drafts is so easy on a word processor that some students produce them copiously. So negotiate with your supervisor how many drafts he or she is prepared to comment on and in what detail. Most supervisors have to set some limits.

Your supervisor and you will have been very close indeed to your work for a number of years. You, in particular, will know it inside out and back to front. So the links between its components may be clear to you, while not being as clear to those who have met your work only recently. It is important to minimize misunderstandings and to find out as early as possible where you are not making yourself clear. Giving departmental seminars will have helped; as will giving conference presentations and writing journal articles. If you have not done any of these recently, then try to find someone new to your work who will listen to you explaining it or will read the draft thesis and tell you where they have trouble following.

You must work through the final draft of the thesis in an editorial mode. Finalizing a thesis is always much more time-consuming than expected. The style must be academic; the text must be written to make a case; chapters have to be linked into a storyline; cross-references and 'pointers' need to be inserted to keep the reader orientated to what is where and why; there should be no typing or stylistic errors; and tables, figures and references should be complete, accurate and presented in whatever format has been agreed with the supervisor.

There may be departmental or institutional guidelines on maximum length. Many require a doctoral thesis not to exceed 100 000 words.

Throughout the writing and editing process, be meticulous about keeping backup copies on floppy disks!

Most students, having word-processed drafts of their theses, choose to prepare their own word-processed final version. Professional typists can, however, support to varying extents, from typing the whole of the thesis, to giving guidance on layout. If you need help, make enquiries well in advance of your deadline, because typists who specialize in theses inevitably find that certain times of the year are busier than others. The departmental secretary or the students' union should be able to make recommendations.

## Presenting the thesis in accordance with institutional requirements

Institutions differ in their requirements for the presentation of a thesis. Fairly standard practice is for there to be a title page (official thesis title, full name of candidate, title of degree and name of institution), followed by an abstract of less than 300 words, a contents page and possibly also a list of diagrams, plates, maps, plans and tables. The normal regulations are that the text should be word-processed or typed using double or $1^1/_2$ line spacing (except for indented quotations and footnotes, which should be single-spaced) on one side only of A4 paper with $1^1/_2$ inch margins, and pages should be numbered continuously from the title page to the end, including all appendices and illustrations. Copyright is normally retained by the author. Institutions and possibly departments normally require a specified number of copies.

In addition to meeting institutional requirements and discipline norms, you need to satisfy yourself and your supervisor. For example, decide how many extra copies of your thesis you will want to keep for yourself and to give to people who have helped you. It is common politeness to give a copy to your supervisor, and to acknowledge him or her formally, along with others who have helped, and it is a nice gesture to include a handwritten note of appreciation in the copy that you give your supervisor.

Use the following activity as a checklist of the salient presentational requirements of your institution.

⬤ **Activity**

What are the requirements of your institution for thesis presentation in terms of the following?

• Numbers of copies

• Paper size, colour and weight

• Fonts and/or typefaces

• Methods of reproduction

• Layout, e.g. margin sizes and line spacing

- Pagination, e.g. of front material as well as of main text

- Style of title page

- Abstract

- Table of contents

- Illustrations, audio and video recordings, etc.

- Binding

- Style of print on binding

- Corrigenda, i.e. how errors may be corrected without retyping and rebinding

Do your institutional regulations require the thesis to be bound for the oral examination?

How long needs to be allowed for a thesis to be bound and how much does it cost?

## Concluding remarks

It is worth finding out early on whether or not the institution requires theses to be bound at the time of the oral examination. Practices vary on this. If regulations allow theses to be unbound, this saves not only time but also money – examiners normally require at least a few amendments to be included in the final bound copies.

Works giving further information on producing a thesis are listed in the Further Reading section.

# 19 PREPARING FOR AND CONDUCTING YOURSELF IN THE EXAMINATION

*Postgraduate research can be seen as a period of uncertainty, ambiguity and lack of structure. The task is not really complete until the oral examination is over.*

(Mathias and Gale, 1991, p. 10)

## The importance of the examination

In the United Kingdom the examination for a research degree is normally in two stages: first, the submission and preliminary assessment of the thesis; and second, its defence by oral examination, also called a viva. Procedures vary from one country to another; in some countries there is no oral examination, while in others it is a very formal public occasion.

In most universities in the United Kingdom, the decision whether or not the thesis is up to the required standard is tentatively taken before the oral examination. However, a poor performance in the oral may lead the examiners to question their decision. This is the main reason why it is in research students' best interests to present themselves as well as they can. Other reasons are that the oral examination can be enjoyable, stimulating and useful. This chapter offers some suggestions for maximizing its potential.

## Entering the examination

With good working relationships between supervisors and research students, there will be a mutual agreement about when a student is ready to enter the examination, although institutional legislation normally lays down that the responsibility belongs to the students. Clearly it would be sensible to go against a supervisor's advice only in very special circumstances.

It is normally research students, not their supervisors, who are responsible for obtaining, completing and delivering entry forms for the examination – and this needs to be thought about several months ahead of time. If the thesis is not submitted within a specified time, the whole entry procedure will have to be repeated.

Some months before your thesis is ready, your supervisor will select an external examiner, who has expertise in your topic, to recommend to the relevant committee of the institution, and he or she will set the formal procedures in motion. While few supervisors would be naive enough to suggest a politically or methodologically incompatible examiner, it is in your own interests, where you can, to involve yourself in the choice. You will know the literature in your field, so suggestions should not come as a surprise, and you may even be able to suggest possibilities. Many supervisors would expect you to, although regulations in some institutions prevent research students from even knowing the names of their examiners in advance.

There will almost certainly also be an internal examiner, but the number and status of examiners depends on the regulations of the institution.

## How oral/viva examinations are conducted

It is normal for oral examinations to take place at research students' home institutions, which external examiners visit. However, there are plans in some places to cut down on the time and costs of travel by arranging the contacts through video link.

An oral examination normally lasts between one and three hours, but it seldom seems this long because everyone gets so involved in the discussion. The external examiner normally chairs and plays the lead role. Being an expert in the topic, he or she is concerned primarily with that topic and with ensuring that standards are as near uniform as possible across institutions. The internal examiner's role is normally more one of organizing and administering the examination, ensuring that it is conducted fairly and that appropriate institutional standards are set and maintained. The internal examiner is likely to be concerned with the student's general knowledge of the wider field and with how the work being examined fits into that field. In some countries the examination is open to the public, and candidates may be expected to give seminars on their work.

---

**Box 19.1** Some general points about orals/vivas

*There is no such thing as a standard viva, but a few general points should be borne in mind. A candidate will not be expected to answer questions from memory and examiners will specify pages or passages in the thesis and allow time to look at them. Usually an examiner will give a general indication of how he or she feels about the thesis including areas of approval or of possible concern. Questions about what worries an examiner should not be taken as a sign that the candidate will be failed, but it is important that they should be answered directly and backed by references to the text of the thesis itself. Finally a candidate should always be prepared to discuss how the work presented by the thesis might be developed further especially for publication.*

(Smith, 1991, p. 56)

---

Many research students prefer not to have their supervisors with them at the oral examination because it can be inhibiting to explain their work in front of someone who knows it so thoroughly already. Supervisors can, however, be present in certain circumstances, depending on institutional regulations. So you should think about whether there are good reasons for this to happen in your case, and then discuss possibilities with your supervisor.

⬛ **Activity**

---

It is sensible to find out as much as possible in advance about what is likely to happen in your oral examination. Ask around to find some answers to the following questions.

• Where will your oral examination take place?

• How long is the examination likely to last?

- How is the examination likely to be conducted?

- Can your supervisor attend, and would you want this to happen?

---

## Preparing yourself for your oral/viva examination

Since the date of the oral may be several months after completion of your work, you will have to reread your thesis some days before, so that it is at your fingertips. An oral examination is often called a thesis defence, and this may help you to prepare better. Reread your thesis, as if trying to find fault. If possible, solicit the aid of a friend. Then prepare suitable defences. Defending is not the same as being defensive. If criticisms seem valid, prepare responses to show that you recognize this by saying what you would have liked to be able to do about them if there were more resources, or what you hope that other workers may still do about them, Box 19.2 suggests some questions to prepare for. It may be helpful to mark your thesis up, using annotated peel-off stickers.

Be prepared for the examiners opening with some simple pleasantries, such as 'What did you enjoy most about your work?' or 'What would you do differently if you were starting out all over again?'. Simple as such questions are, unless you prepare for them, they may throw you and affect how you conduct yourself in the rest of the examination.

---

**Box 19.2**  Some questions to prepare for

(a) The 'context' of your research – which debates, issues, problems it is addressing.
(b) The 'red thread' of your research – the idea that binds it together.
(c) Its main findings, i.e. your (major) contribution(s) to knowledge.

It is one of the classic opening gambits of external examiners, after an initial question to set the candidate at ease, to ask a question along these lines.

(Clark, 1991, p. 45)

Also be prepared for the examiners to ask you to present parts of your work orally. They often do this to check that a thesis is the research student's own work and to gauge his or her understanding of it.

You may also like to prepare some questions for the examiners, although whether or not you actually use them should be a matter of judgement at the time. You will certainly want to impress with the quality of your thinking, but it would be unwise to raise issues to which they might not be able to respond readily. Suitable questions might concern information which they might have on recent related work elsewhere or advice on how to go about publishing your work.

Once you know who your examiners will be, it is sensible to find out what you can about them. You should certainly familiarize yourself with their work and find links between it and your own. If at all possible, ask around to find out their examination style.

You will want to be in good form for the examination. Do not think that drugs, or alcohol or chewing gum will relax the tension. They will not. There is some evidence that they make performance worse, and they will probably lower the examiners' view of you. A clean handkerchief is good insurance, to wipe sweaty palms and even tears, but any tension should disappear rapidly once discussion gets under way.

(■)  **Activity**

---

What can you find out about your external examiner's examining style?

What can you find out about your external examiner's work?

What can you usefully find out about your internal examiner?

With the aid of staff and other research students, develop a set of simple questions that examiners are likely to use to open proceedings.

Prepare responses to these questions, oriented towards giving the impression that you are thoughtful and honest and that you appreciate what a research degree ought to be about.

Read through your thesis as if you were an examiner trying to criticize aspects of it, and develop a defence. Check this out, preferably with your supervisor, to make sure that it is reasonable and not defensive.

Prepare – with due sensitivity – some questions to ask or issues to raise with the examiners.

## Setting up tokens of appreciation

In some departments, it may be a normal courtesy to give some small token of appreciation to a supervisor, or to put on a celebration for other students. These may have to be set up in advance of the examination, even at the risk of tempting fate.

 **Activity**

You will probably already know the normal practice in the department for showing appreciation to examiners, the supervisor, and other staff and students. If not, find out, and then adapt it to suit yourself.

## Dressing for the oral/viva examination

For a typical oral examination, you would be well advised to choose clothes that are smart and businesslike, to show that you appreciate the importance of the occasion. The exception is where the external examiner is likely to be scruffy – effectively a form of 'uniform' in some areas of academia and with certain academics. Be guided by what is known about the way the examiners tend to dress, and do not upstage them. Whatever style of dress you eventually think fitting to adopt, choose your outfit with care and make sure that it is comfortable.

It may help to ask a friend to check over your outfit with you and spend time discussing options. If you have nothing suitable, consider buying or borrowing. Think about whether you would give a better impression if you did your hair differently – this applies to both sexes!

## Conducting yourself in the oral/viva examination

Although it is understandable that you may be nervous at the prospect of the oral examination, most students find that they enjoy the experience of discussing their work with able and informed individuals. Remember, you are the world's expert on your work, and your supervisor and the resources of your department should have provided you with sound support throughout your period as a research student; if you are not considered ready to be examined, you should have been told – and if you are considered ready, everything should go smoothly.

There are, however, a few guidelines on conducting yourself:

- If you think better when you jot things down, take a pen and paper along with the copy of your thesis.
- Act with composure. Say good morning or good afternoon when you enter the room, but do not speak again until you are spoken to, or until the discussion reaches the stage of exhilarated debate. The examiners will want you to be pleasant but they will not be impressed by gregariousness.
- Sit squarely on the chair, not poised on the edge. If there is anything about the room arrangement that disturbs you, ask politely for it to be changed.
- Show that you are listening attentively to the examiners' questions. They will expect you to argue, but try to do so without emotion, on the basis of evidence and keeping personalities out of it, showing that you take others' points of view seriously, even if you do not agree with them. If you are in doubt, ask for clarification. Do not defend every point; be prepared to concede some, but not too many.

## Preparing for the result

It is not unknown for examiners to say at the beginning of the oral examination that the candidate has passed. Many examiners, however, would never consider doing so, in that it would invalidate the whole purpose of the examination. Normally if everything goes smoothly, you will be told after the oral that you have passed, subject as always to ratification by the institution.

In even the best theses, examiners often want small amendments of the sort which can be made directly on existing pages or stuck in. The supervisor, in conjunction with one of the examiners, is usually given the responsibility of ensuring that this work is carried out satisfactorily, without further formal examination.

If more substantial changes are required, or additional work needs to be done, the thesis may be required to be examined again at a later date. The student is given a specified time to do this, normally about 18 months – but it is advisable to do it as soon as possible while the work is still fresh in one's mind.

The examiners have a number of other options, depending on the regulations of the institution. These include failing the thesis completely or awarding an MPhil instead of a PhD, if they feel that the thesis does not merit the award of a doctorate.

# 20 AFTERWARDS!

*Life can only be understood backwards, but it must be lived forwards.*
>                               (Søren Kierkegaard, quoted in Stephenson 1967)

Having got as far as the examination, it is normal to pass, even if the examiners require certain amendments to the thesis. If you are asked to make amendments, it is best to deal with them quickly, while the work is still fresh in your mind, even if you do not feel in the least like it. In the very rare case of anything going seriously wrong, students' unions can normally supply professional advisers to advise on appeals.

You may expect that you will feel elated at your success. Other emotions, however, are not unknown, because the emotional buildup has been so great. A common emotion is detachment, as if this great thing has not really happened. Another is lack of purpose because a driving force of your life over a number of years has been severed. After a while, though, looking back on the experience of being a research student, you can expect to feel proud of your achievement. You can also expect a sense of personal confidence in having become uniquely knowledgeable in your chosen area.

As soon as you can after the examination take a short holiday, to mark the end of your time as a research student, and to refresh yourself for getting on with the next stage of your life. If you would like this to include publishing your research, either as a book or in the form of several journal articles, your supervisor will doubtless help. The Further Reading section gives a suitable reference.

Once you begin your career, the skills developed during your research programme will prove invaluable. This is not only true of those relating directly to research in your discipline area, valuable as these may be. The personal and transferable skills are equally important (see Boxes 20.1 and 20.2) and will prove their worth even if your career develops outside your current discipline area.

---

**Box 20.1** Skills for succeeding in your career

The following comment is from the co-author of 'Skills for the 21st Century', a report by the Association of Graduate Employers.

*Will graduates need IT skills? Of course they will. Will they need foreign language skills? Of course they will. But will those skills be the defining skills of the 21st century? I don't think so. The skills for the future include self-promotion, action planning, networking, coping with uncertainty and 'political awareness' – or an understanding of the hidden tensions and power struggles within organisations.*

(Jonathan Winter, as reported by Simon Targett in
*Times Higher Education Supplement*, 1995, p. 5)

---

**Box 20.2** Planning a career is about grasping opportunities

The following is from a review of the book *Roads to the Top: Career Decisions and Development of 18 Business Leaders* by Ruth Tait.

*Career planning for those in the fast lane is not scientific. It is mostly to do with spotting and taking advantage of opportunities.*

(Mileham, 1995)

# FURTHER READING

*If I have seen further, it is by standing on the shoulders of giants.*
(Sir Isaac Newton, letter to Robert Hooke)

All research students should read widely. This section lists some of the best-known, tried and tested material, which all research students would do well to consult, irrespective of their field of study. Even where a specific discipline appears in the title, usefulness is not limited to that discipline.

The list cannot be full and comprehensive because new material is constantly becoming available. Probably one of the best ways of using the list is to locate the location/classification numbers of its items in your institutional library, and then also browse through titles which are adjacently shelved. You may also find it useful to refer to the items in the next section, the Select Bibliography. This lists major works consulted in the preparation of the book.

No general reading list can ever be a substitute for the advice of supervisors and other researchers in your own specific field.

## General

Bell, J. (1993) *Doing Your Research Project* (2nd edition), Buckingham: Open University Press.
Calnan, J. (1984) *Coping with Research: The Complete Guide for Beginners*, London: William Heinemann Medical.
Howard, K. and Sharp, J. (1983) *The Management of a Student Research Project*, Aldershot: Gower.
Madsen, D. (1983) *Successful Dissertations and Theses: A Guide to Graduate Student Research from Proposal to Completion*, San Francisco: Jossey Bass.
National Postgraduate Committee (1995) *The Postgraduate Book* (2nd edition), Brandon House, Troon, Ayrshire, KA10 6HX.

Phillips, E. and Pugh, D. (1994) *How to get a PhD* (2nd edition), Buckingham: Open University Press.
Rudestam, K. and Newton, R. (1992) *Surviving your Dissertation*, London: Sage.
Salmon, P. (1992) *Achieving a PhD – Ten Students' Experiences*, Stoke-on-Trent: Trentham Books.

## 1 Introduction

On study skills at undergraduate and taught masters level:

Fairbairn, G. and Winch, C. (1993) *Reading, Writing and Reasoning*, Buckingham: Society for Research into Higher Education and Open University Press.
Freeman, R. and Meed, J. (1993) *How to Study Effectively*, Hammersmith: CollinsEducational.
Hector Taylor, M. and Bonsall, M. (eds) (1993) *Successful Study*, Sheffield: Hallamshire Press.
Maddox, H. (1988) *How to Study*, London: Pan.
Rowntree, D. (1988) *Learn How to Study*, London: Warner.

On research design:
The works listed above in the General section also include guidance on research design.

## 2 Registering for a research degree

See publications from various institutions.

## 3 Preparing for the way of life of a research student

On being a part-time student:
Bourner, T. and Race, P. (1990) *How to Win as a Part-time Student*, London: Kogan Page.

On being a woman student:
Vartuli, S. (ed.) (1982) *The PhD Experience: A Woman's Point of View*, New York: Praeger.

## 4 Settling in as a new research student

On office accommodation:
Gross, B. (1994) 'Accommodation of Research Students', *Journal of Graduate Education*, 1, 1, 21–4.

National Postgraduate Committee (1995) *Guidelines on Accommodation and Facilities for Postgraduate Research*, Brandon House, Troon, Ayrshire, KA10 6HX.

## 5 Towards recognizing good research

On the nature of the PhD in different disciplines (for interest only – be guided by your supervisor for research in your discipline area):
Advisory Board for the Research Councils (1993) *The Nature of the PhD*, London: ABRC.

On different approaches to research and research methodology, and dealing with subjectivity:
Denzin, N. and Lincoln, Y. (eds) (1994) *Handbook of Qualitative Research*. Beverly Hills, CA: Sage.
Guba, E. and Lincoln, Y. (1988) 'Do Inquiry Paradigms Imply Inquiry Methodologies?' In Fetterman, D. (ed.) *Qualitative Approaches to Evaluation in Education*, New York: Praeger.
Saloman, G. (1991) 'Transcending the Qualitative–Quantitative Debate: The Anatomy of Systematic Approaches to Educational Research', *Educational Researcher*, 20, 6, 10–18.

On research design:
The works listed above in the General section also include guidance on research design.

On compiling arguments, counter-arguments and discussion:
Fairbairn, G. and Winch, C. (1993) *Reading, Writing and Reasoning*, Buckingham: Society for Research into Higher Education and Open University Press.
Pirie, D. (1991) *How to Write Critical Essays*, London: Routledge.

On procedures for style and documentation in writing up research:
Turabian, K. (1982) *A Manual for Writers of Research Papers, Theses and Dissertations*, London: Heinemann.

## 6 Interacting with your supervisor(s)

On being assertive when dealing with people:
Back, K. and Back, K. (1982) *Assertiveness at Work*, London: McGraw-Hill.

On supervisory practices:
Economic and Social Research Council (undated) *The Preparation and Supervision of Research Theses in the Social Sciences*. Swindon: Economic and Social Research Council.

Science and Engineering Research Council (1989) *Research Student and Supervisor: An Approach to Good Supervisory Practice*, Swindon: Science and Engineering Research Council.
National Postgraduate Committee (1995) *Guidelines for Codes of Practice for Postgraduate Research*, Brandon House, Troon, Ayrshire, KA10 6HX. First printed 1992.

On appeal procedures:
National Postgraduate Committee (1995) *Guidelines for the Conduct of Research Degree Appeals*, Brandon House, Troon, Ayrshire, KA10 6HX.

## 7 Keeping records

The books in the General section also give some advice on keeping records.

## 8 Planning ahead

Lock, D. (1989) *Project Management*, Aldershot: Gower.

## 9 Managing yourself and your time

The books in the General section also give advice on managing your own time. In addition, there is no shortage of books on time management generally, but these need to be adapted for the particular circumstances of research students.

On taking on teaching work:
National Postgraduate Committee (1994) *Guidelines for Employment of Postgraduate Students as Teachers*, Brandon House, Troon, Ayrshire, KA10 6HX.

## 10 Taking responsibility for your own progress

The books in the General section also give advice on managing your own progress.

## 11 Cooperating with others for mutual help and support

On asserting oneself with others:
Back, K. and Back, K. (1982) *Assertiveness at Work*, London: McGraw-Hill.

On intellectual property rights:
Association of University Teachers – National Association of Teachers in Further and Higher Education Confederation (1995) *Intellectual Property in the Workplace*, London: AUT-NATFHE.

## 12 Producing reports

Blicq, R. S. (1987) *Writing Reports to Get Results: Guidelines for the Computer Age*, New York: Electrical and Electronic Engineers Press.

## 13 Giving presentations on your work

Hamlin, D. (1989) *How to Talk So People Listen*, Wellingborough: Thorsons.
Tufte, E. R. (1983) *The Visual Display of Quantitative Information*, Cheshire, CT: Graphics Press.

## 14 Landmarks, hurdles and transferring from MPhil to PhD

On the nature of the landmarks and institutional procedures:
See publications from various institutions.

On writing and structuring reports:
Barrass, R. (1991) *Scientists Must Write*, London: Chapman & Hall.
Becker, H. (1986) *Writing for Social Scientists*, Chicago: University of Chicago Press.
Blicq, R. S. (1987) *Writing Reports to Get Results: Guidelines for the Computer Age*, New York: Electrical and Electronic Engineers Press.
Day, R. A. (1988) *How to Write and Publish a Scientific Paper* (3rd edition), Cambridge: Cambridge University Press.

On compiling arguments, counter-arguments and discussion:
Fairbairn, G. and Winch, C. (1993) *Reading, Writing and Reasoning*, Buckingham: Society for Research into Higher Education and Open University Press.
Pirie, D. (1991) *How to Write Critical Essays*, London: Routledge.

On procedures for style and documentation in writing up research:
Turabian, K. (1982) *A Manual for Writers of Research Papers, Theses and Dissertations*, London: Heinemann.

## 15 Coming to terms with originality in research

Phillips, E. and Pugh, D. (1994) *How to get a PhD* (2nd edition), Buckingham: Open University Press.

## 16 Developing skills for creative thinking

Buzan, T. (1977) *Use Your Head*, London: BBC Publications.
De Bono, E. (1991) *Serious Creativity*, London: HarperCollins.
Kemp, R. and Race, P. (1992) 'Promoting the Development of Personal and Professional Skills'. Module 10 of Cryer, P. (ed.) *Effective Learning and Teaching in Higher Education*, Sheffield: Universities' Staff Development Unit.

## 17 Dealing with flagging

Salmon, P. (1992) *Achieving a PhD – Ten Students' Experiences*, Stoke-on-Trent: Trentham Books.
Fontana, D. (1993) *Managing Stress*, Leicester: British Psychological Society and Routledge.

## 18 Producing your thesis

On writing and structuring reports:
Barrass, R. (1991) *Scientists Must Write*, London: Chapman & Hall.
Becker, H. (1986) *Writing for Social Scientists*, Chicago: University of Chicago Press.
Blicq, R. S. (1987) *Writing Reports to Get Results: Guidelines for the Computer Age*, New York: Electrical and Electronic Engineers Press.
Day, R. A. (1988) *How to Write and Publish a Scientific Paper* (3rd edition), Cambridge: Cambridge University Press.

On compiling argument, counter-argument and discussion:
Fairbairn, G. and Winch, C. (1993) *Reading, Writing and Reasoning*, Buckingham: Society for Research into Higher Education and Open University Press.
Pirie, D. (1991) *How to Write Critical Essays*, London: Routledge.

On procedures for style and documentation in writing up research:
Turabian, K. (1982) *A Manual for Writers of Research Papers, Theses and Dissertations*, London: Heinemann.

## 19 Preparing for and conducting yourself in the examination

On the oral examination:
Burnham, P. (1994) 'Surviving the Viva: Unravelling the Mysteries of the PhD Oral', *Journal of Graduate Education*, 1, 1, 30–34.

On dealing with people assertively:
Back, K. and Back, K. (1982) *Assertiveness at Work*, London: McGraw-Hill.

## 20 Afterwards!

On turning the thesis into a book:
Harman, E. and Montagnes, I. (eds) (1976) *The Thesis and the Book*, Toronto: Toronto University Press.

On appeal procedures:
National Postgraduate Committee (1995) *Guidelines for the Conduct of Research Degree Appeals*, Brandon House, Troon, Ayrshire, KA10 6HX.

# SELECT BIBLIOGRAPHY

This Select Bibliography contains the more significant works consulted during the preparation of the book which are not listed in the References.

Advisory Board for the Research Councils (1993) *The Nature of the PhD*, London: ABRC.

Allan, G. and Skinner, C. (eds) (1991) *Handbook for Research Students in the Social Sciences*, Brighton: Falmer Press.

Back, K. and Back, K. (1982) *Assertiveness at Work*, London: McGraw-Hill.

Barrass, R. (1991) *Scientists Must Write*, London: Chapman & Hall.

Becher, T., Henkel, M. and Kogan, M. (1994) *Graduate Education in Britain*, London: Jessica Kingsley.

Becker, H. (1986) *Writing for Social Scientists*, Chicago: University of Chicago Press.

Bell, J. (1993) *Doing Your Research Project* (2nd edition), Buckingham: Open University Press.

Bennect, R. and Knubbs, J. (1986) 'Researching for a Higher Degree: The Role(s) of the Supervisor', *Management Education and Development*, 17, 2, 137–45.

Blicq, R. S. (1987) *Writing Reports to Get Results: Guidelines for the Computer Age*, New York: Electrical and Electronic Engineers Press.

Bourner, T. and Race, P. (1990) *How to Win as a Part-time Student*, London: Kogan Page.

Bourner, T. and Hughes, M. (1991) 'Joint Supervision of Research Degrees', *Higher Education Review*, 24, 21–34.

Bowen, W. and Rudenstine, N. (1992) *In Pursuit of the PhD*, Princeton, NJ: Princeton University Press.

Bruce, S. (1994) 'Research Students' Early Experiences of the Dissertation Literature Review', *Studies in Higher Education*, 19, 2, 217–29.

Burgess, R. (ed.) (1994) *Postgraduate Education and Training in the Social Sciences: Processes and Products*, London: Jessica Kingsley.

Burnham, P. (1994) 'Surviving the Viva: Unravelling the Mysteries of the PhD Oral', *Journal of Graduate Education*, 1, 1, 30–4.

Buzan, T. (1977) *Use Your Head*, London: BBC Publications.

Calnan, J. (1984) *Coping with Research: The Complete Guide for Beginners*, London: William Heinemann Medical.

Committee of Vice-Chancellors and Principals/Committee of Directors of Polytechnics (1992) *The Management of Higher Degrees Undertaken by Overseas Students*, London: CVCP/CDP.

Day, R. A. (1988) *How to Write and Publish a Scientific Paper* (3rd edition), Cambridge: Cambridge University Press.

Denicolo, P., Entwistle, N. and Hounsell, D. (1992) 'What is Active Learning?' Module 1 of Cryer, P. (ed.) *Effective Learning and Teaching in Higher Education*, Sheffield: Universities' Staff Development Unit.

Economic and Social Research Council (undated) *Postgraduate Training*, Swindon: Economic and Social Research Council.

Elton, L. and Pope, M. (1989) 'Research Supervision: The Value of Collegiality', *Cambridge Journal of Education*, 19, 267–76.

Fairbairn, G. and Winch, C. (1993) *Reading, Writing and Reasoning*, Buckingham: Society for Research into Higher Education and Open University Press.

Freeman, R. and Meed, J. (1993) *How to Study Effectively*, Hammersmith: CollinsEducational.

Guba, E. and Lincoln, Y. (1988) 'Do Inquiry Paradigms Imply Inquiry Methodologies?' In Fetterman, D. (ed.) *Qualitative Approaches to Evaluation in Education*, New York: Praeger.

Guba, E. (1978) *Towards a Methodology of Naturalistic Enquiry*, Los Angeles: Center for the Study of Education.

Hamilton, J. (ed.) (1990) *They Made Our World*, London: BBC Publications.

Hamlin, D. (1989) *How to Talk So People Listen*, Wellingborough: Thorsons.

Hampson, L. (1994) *How's Your Dissertation Going?* Lancaster: Unit for Innovation in Higher Education.

Harman, E. and Montagnes, I. (eds) (1976) *The Thesis and the Book*, Toronto: Toronto University Press.

Hector Taylor, M. and Bonsall, M. (eds) (1993) *Successful Study*, Sheffield: Hallamshire Press.

HMSO (1976) *British Standard 1629: Recommendations for Bibliographical References*, London: HMSO.

HMSO (1978) *British Standard 5605: Recommendations Citing Publications by Bibliographical References*, London: HMSO.

HMSO (1990) *British Standard 4821: Recommendations for the Presentation of Theses*, London: HMSO.

Howard, K. and Sharp, J. (1983) *The Management of a Student Research Project*, Aldershot: Gower.

Katz, J. and Hartnett, R. (eds) (1976) *Scholars in the Making*, Cambridge, MA: Ballinger.

Kemp, R. and Race, P. (1992) 'Promoting the Development of Personal and Professional Skills'. Module 10 of Cryer, P. (ed.) *Effective Learning and Teaching in Higher Education*, Sheffield: Universities' Staff Development Unit.

Kirkman, J. (1975) 'That Pernicious Passive Voice', *Physics in Technology*, September, 197–200.

Lock, D. (1989) *Project Management*, Aldershot: Gower.

Maddox, H. (1988) *How to Study*, London: Pan.

Madsen, D. (1983) *Successful Dissertations and Theses: A Guide to Graduate Student Research from Proposal to Completion*, San Francisco: Jossey Bass.

Moses, I. (1984) 'Supervision of Higher Degree Students – Problem Areas and Possible Solutions', *Higher Education Research and Development*, 3, 2, 153–65.

Moses, I. (1985) *Supervising Postgraduates*, Kensington, NSW: Higher Education Research and Development Society of Australasia.

National Postgraduate Committee (1994) *Annual Report 1993–1994*, Brandon House, Troon, Ayrshire, KA10 6HX.

National Postgraduate Committee (1994) *Guidelines for Employment of Postgraduate Students as Teachers*, Brandon House, Troon, Ayrshire, KA10 6HX.

National Postgraduate Committee (1995) *Guidelines for the Conduct of Research Degree Appeals*, Brandon House, Troon, Ayrshire, KA10 6HX.

National Postgraduate Committee (1995) *Guidelines on Accommodation and Facilities for Postgraduate Research*, Brandon House, Troon, Ayrshire, KA10 6HX.

Noble, K. (1994) *Changing Doctoral Degrees: An International Perspective*, Buckingham: Society for Research into Higher Education and Open University Press.

Office of Science and Technology (1994) *Consultative Document: A New Structure for Postgraduate Research Training Supported by the Research Councils*, London: HMSO.

Patton, M. Q. (1990) *Qualitative Evaluation and Research Methods*, Beverly Hills, CA: Sage.

Phillips, E. (1991) 'Learning to Do Research'. In Smith, N. and Dainty, D. (eds) *The Management Research Handbook*, London: Routledge.

Phillips, E. (1994) 'Avoiding Communication Breakdown'. In Zuber-Skerritt, O. and Ryan, Y. (eds) *Quality in Postgraduate Education*, London: Kogan Page.

Phillips, E. and Pugh, D. (1994) *How to get a PhD* (2nd edition), Buckingham: Open University Press.

Pope, M. and Gilbert, J. (1984) 'Doing Research into Teaching and Learning: Module L of Diploma in the Practice of Higher Education', IED University of Surrey internal publication.

Pratt, J. M. (1984) 'Writing Your Thesis', *Chemistry in Britain*, 20, 1114–15.

Rist, R. (1977) 'On the Relations among Educational Paradigms: From Distain to Detente', *Anthropology and Education Quarterly*, 8, 42–9.

Rowntree, D. (1988) *Learn How to Study*, London: Warner.

Rudestam, K. and Newton, R. (1992) *Surviving Your Dissertation*, London: Sage.

Stephenson, B. (ed.) (1967) *Home Book of Quotations: Classical and Modern*, New York: Dood, Mead.

Tripp, R. (1976) *The International Thesaurus of Quotations*, Harmonsworth: Penguin.

Tufte, E. R. (1983) *The Visual Display of Quantitative Information*, Cheshire, CT: Graphics Press.

Turabian, K. (1982) *A Manual for Writers of Research Papers, Theses and Dissertations*, London: Heinemann.

Vartuli, S. (ed.) (1982) *The PhD Experience: A Woman's Point of View*, New York: Praeger.

Watson, G. (1970) *The Literary Thesis: a Guide to Research*, London: Longman.

Welsh, J. M. (1979) *The First Year of Postgraduate Study*, Guildford: Society for Research into Higher Education.

Williams, K. (1989) *Study Skills*, Basingstoke: Macmillan.

Wright, J. and Lodwick, R. (1989) 'The Process of the PhD: A Study of the First Year of Doctoral Study', *Research Papers in Education*, 4, 22–56.

Youngman, M. B. (1989) *Role Expectations of Research Supervisors and Students: Final Report R231786*, Swindon: Economic and Social Research Council.

# REFERENCES

Australian Vice-Chancellors' Committee (1990) *Guidelines for Responsible Practice in Research and Dealing with Problems of Research Misconduct.* Deakin, Vic.: Australian Vice-Chancellors' Committee.

Bargar, R. and Duncan, J. (1982) 'Cultivating Creative Endeavour in Doctoral Research', *Journal of Higher Education*, 53, 1, 1–31.

Becher, T. Henkel, M. and Kogan, M. (1995) *Graduate Education and Staffing: Report of a Research Seminar*, London: Committee of Vice-Chancellors and Principals/Society for Reseach into Higher Education.

Berry, R. (1986) *How to Write a Research Paper*, Oxford: Pergamon.

Bowrick, P. (1995) 'Blowing the Whistle on Referees', *Times Higher Education Supplement*, 10 February, p. 11.

Bristow, J. (1995) 'Teachers and Petting Do Not Mix', *Times Higher Education Supplement*, 2 June, p. 12.

Clark, D. (1995) Foreword, *Journal of Graduate Education*, 1, 4, 101–2.

Clark, J. (1991) 'Personal Views'. In Allan, G. and Skinner, C. (eds) *Handbook for Research Students in the Social Sciences*, Brighton: Falmer Press.

Cryer, P. (1996) 'Training Research Students and Supporting Supervisors through Self-study Materials Customised for the Research Student, *The Journal of Graduate Education*, 2, 2, 44–52.

Denzin, N. and Lincoln, Y. (eds) (1994) *Handbook of Qualitative Research.* Beverly Hills, CA: Sage.

Economic and Social Research Council (1986) *The Preparation and Supervision of Research Theses in the Social Sciences.* Swindon: Economic and Social Research Council.

Ehrenberg, A. (1982) Writing technical papers or reports, *The American Statistician*, 36, 4, 326–9.

Engineering and Physical Sciences Research Council (1995) *Postgraduate Research: A Guide to Good Supervisory Practice, Consultative Document, August 1995*, Swindon: Engineering and Physical Sciences Research Council.

Eysenk, H. (1994) 'Past Masters: Hans Eysenck Describes His Unsympathetic Mentor, Sir Cyril Burt', *Times Higher Education Supplement*, 14 October, p. 17.

Fontana, D. (1993) *Managing Stress*, Leicester: British Psychological Society and Routledge.

Francis, J. (1976) 'Supervision and Examination of Higher Degree Students', *Bulletin of the University of London*, 31, 3–6.

Gross, B. (1994) 'The Accommodation of Research Students', *Journal of Graduate Education*, 1, 1, 21–4.

Heisenberg, W. (1971) *Physics and Beyond: Encounters and Conversations*, translated by A. J. Pomerans, New York: Harper & Row.

Hockey, J. (1994) 'New Territory: Problems of Adjusting to the First Year of a Social Science PhD', *Studies in Higher Education*, 19, 2, 177–90.

McArthur, T. (1992) *The Oxford Companion to the English Language*, Oxford: Oxford University Press.

Martin, J. (1982) 'A Garbage can model of the research process'. In McGrath, M. *et al. Judgment Calls in Research*, Beverly Hills, CA: Sage.

Mathias, H. and Gale, T. (1991) 'Undertaking a Research Degree'. In Allen, G. and Skinner, C. (eds) *Handbook for Research Students in the Social Sciences*, Brighton: Falmer Press.

Medawar, P. (1981) *Advice to a Young Scientist*, London: Pan.

Mileham, P. (1995) 'Executive Cases in Brief', *Times Higher Education Supplement*, 24 November, p. 32.

National Postgraduate Committee (1993) *The Postgraduate Book*, Brandon House, Troon, Ayrshire, KA10 6HX.

National Postgraduate Committee (1995) *Guidelines for Codes of Practice for Postgraduate Research* (2nd edition), Brandon House, Troon, Ayrshire, KA10 6HX.

Parry, S. and Hayden, M. (1994) *Supervising Higher Degree Research Students: An Investigation of Practices across a Range of Academic Departments*, Canberra: Australian Government Publishing Service.

Pirie, D. (1991) *How to Write Critical Essays*, London: Routledge.

*Prima Magazine*, October 1994, p. 57.

Salmon, P. (1992) *Achieving a PhD – Ten Students' Experiences*, Stoke-on-Trent: Trentham Books.

Science and Engineering Research Council (1992) *Research Student and Supervisor: An Approach to Good Supervisory Practice*, Swindon: Science and Engineering Research Council.

Shatner, W. (1993) *Star Trek Memories*, London: HarperCollins.

Smith, J. (1991) 'What Are Examiners Looking For?' In Allan, G. and Skinner, C. (eds) *Handbook for Research Students in the Social Sciences*, Brighton: Falmer Press.

Targett, S. (1995) 'More Money than Job Skills', *Times Higher Education Supplement*, 13 October, p. 5.

*Times Higher Education Supplement* (1995) Lecturers told to Dampen Ardour, *THES*, 2 June, p. 4.

UK Council for Graduate Education (1995) *Graduate Schools*, Warwick: UK Council for Graduate Education.

University College London Graduate School (1994) *Graduate Society Newsletter*, Issue 1.

Wilkins, B. (1995) Personal communication.

Zuber-Skerritt, O. and Ryan, Y. (eds) (1994) *Quality in Postgraduate Education*, London: Kogan Page.

# USEFUL ADDRESSES

The following are addresses of non-discipline-specific organizations in the United Kingdom which are concerned with the support of postgraduate research students and/or postgraduate research policy.

The National Postgraduate Committee
Brandon House
Bentinck Drive
Troon
Ayrshire KA10 6HX

UK Council for Graduate Education
c/o CEDAR
University of Warwick
Coventry CV4 7AL

The Council for International Education (UKCOSA)
9–17 St Albans Place
London N1 0NX

LIBRARY
EDUCATION CENTRE
PRINCESS ROYAL HOSPITAL

# INDEX

## HOW TO GET A PHD (2nd edition)
A HANDBOOK FOR STUDENTS AND THEIR SUPERVISORS

## Estelle M. Phillips and D. S. Pugh

This is a handbook and survival manual for PhD students, providing a practical, realistic understanding of the processes of doing research for a doctorate. It discusses many important issues often left unconsidered, such as the importance of time management and how to achieve it, and how to overcome the difficulties of communicating with supervisors. Consideration is given to the particular problems of groups such as women, part-time and overseas students.

The book also provides practical insights for supervisors, focusing on how to monitor and, if necessary, improve supervisory practice. It assists senior academic administrators by examining the responsibilities that universities have for providing an adequate service for research students. This is a revised and updated second edition; it will be as warmly welcomed as the first edition:

> One way of providing a more supportive environment for PhD students is for supervisors to recommend this book.
>
> *(Teaching News)*

> Warmly recommended as a bedside companion, both to those hoping to get a PhD and to those who have the responsibility of guiding them, often with very little support themselves.
>
> *(Higher Education Review)*

> This is an excellent book. Its style is racy and clear . . . an impressive array of information, useful advice and comment gleaned from the authors' systematic study and experience over many years . . . should be required reading not only for those contemplating doctoral study but also for all supervisors, new and experienced.
>
> *(Higher Education)*

### Contents

224pp    0 335 19214 9 (Paperback)

STAFFORD
UNIVERS
LIBRARY